YO-CAV-231

A Reluctant Immigrant

A Memoir & Menu

by

Felizitas Sudendorf

Helgard Press · Chicago

HELGARD PRESS

Copyright © 2012 by Felizitas Sudendorf

All rights reserved.

Published in the United States by Helgard Press

ISBN: 978-0-9848049-5-5

Printed in the United States of America

Cover design by Kelly Hyde

First Edition

I wish to dedicate this book to the persons
who've had the biggest influence on my life;
my mother Benigna and my children
Patricia, Linda, Maria, Richard and Alex.

A Reluctant Immigrant

A Memoir & Menu

Prologue

The motivation behind this memoir is to feed my grand-children's constant hunger for stories of my childhood. Whenever I babysit, we have a routine at bedtime to each tell a story after prayer. The doors to all the bedrooms open so that we can hear one another and the lights go out. Each one of us has a turn to say what's on his or her mind or tell a fantastic story. When it's my turn, they tell me right from the start "…and, Oma, don't tell us a 'Once upon a time story…' tell us stories about when you were a little girl and why you came to America."

And so, while my mind is still, for the most part working, I thought I would attempt to write down my family's story – for my children, grandchildren, and anyone else whose journey has taken them to this great country of ours. I didn't always think it was all that great.

Well, let me think, where should I begin? First, some neces-sary background...

Many generations ago at the start of the 19th century – about 1809, my ancestors were farmers in the Black Forest region of

Germany, an area often plagued by war. At about that time a call went out from Russia to German farmers to come populate and work the vast steppes. The Russian monarchy at that time was of German lineage and so the prospect did not seem too impossible and this would certainly increase their agricultural presence. However, once these farms were established, only one child could inherit the family farm, as was the custom at that time. Since most farmers had large families and land was scarce, many of the younger siblings were prone to wanderlust.

As a result, people from nearly all the western provinces of Germany were on the move with horse and wagon in search of a new beginning for their own promised land. Across Europe a migration took place, first through Prussia then to Russia, onto southern Ukraine, to Besserabia, and finally to the Dobrudja in Rumania on the Black Sea. My great-great-great grandfather, Ludwig Mueller, heeded that call, leaving Gerlingen in Württemberg about that time. The journey spanned several generations of roaming from country to country. This is where my story begins.

My maternal great grandparents Jacob and Appolonia Bachmeier were born in Krasna, Bessarabia. For their family and scores of others, saying it was hard at first is an understatement. No knowledge of the language was the most significant impediment. As with most immigrants, they had to build everything from the bottom up, often with large families to feed and clothe and provide a home. For the first several years they had to overcome poor harvests and brutal winters, yet slowly this new place had become home. They had made it and felt at peace, or... so they thought.

War broke out between Russia and Turkey, which brought about new uncertainties for the farmers; making them pull out stakes again, leaving everything behind and heading south along the Black Sea to Turkish-occupied, Rumania. After the last of the many conflicts, Turkish farmers returned from Rumania to their homeland, leaving their houses and lands vacant. German farmers settled into this land and started rebuilding once again. My family set down stakes in a small town named Karamurat, near Constanza. Here my mother's parents, Basilius and Felicia Ruschiensky, my father's parents Aloisius and Marianne Mueller were born, as were my parents Mathias and Benigna Mueller and my younger sister Perpetua and I.

These newly-landed farmers built whitewashed farmhouses and their own school and church. The bricks for the church were made out of mud, straw and sand. Everything was made by their own hands and with their own industrious know-how. They built a community with straight roads and trees along each side, behind which sat the fruits of their labor: farmhouses, large courtyards, barns, stables with many horses and their beloved wine cellars. The farmers prospered here for three generations – with families having eight to ten children, the population multiplied quickly. Though many babies died in childbirth or shortly thereafter, still many survived. Village elders sought to ensure every member of the community – rich or poor – made it through the seasons. The widows and their children most especially, needed to be taken care of.

The women had not much leisure time. Raising large families, cooking, harvesting, washing with no running water, milking the cows, making butter and cheese, making sausages after their husbands slaughtered the pig or lamb for the holidays, this was their accepted life. They had, at last, something to call their own – a community within a village made up of Rumanians, Tartars and Germans – living in harmony. The families, however, were their greatest source of joy and accomplishment. It seemed as though all were able to rejoice and celebrate. And they did so with their beautiful voices; singing often and with much gusto.

The young men and women who were not necessarily talented in farming were sent to the capital city of Bucharest for studies. The religious convents and monasteries were the most sought after places of learning and produced many splendid novices, priests and teachers who in turn, provided a source of great pride for the family back in Karamurat.

With little money, trading and bartering – goods for goods – was the norm. As farmers, we could always count on the city merchant, Mr. Edelstein, for provisions; coffee, sugar, etc. in exchange for whatever that particular farm had to offer. On one particular trip to Mr. Edelstein, one farmer was told not to frequent this merchant any longer because this place was being watched and customers may be implicated. This did not sit well with the farmers, who treated the news with disbelief. Not long after, war broke out; and for these German people and for this particular clan of German farmers, this did not bode well. World War II was coming to them.

A call went out for all German people to leave Rumania. Although they were Rumanian citizens, they had to leave. Where could they go? Who would have them? Their original homeland would have to take them, no? The people were crushed, leaving everything behind – everything they had so feverishly worked for – taking only what they could carry. This could not be happening. For people who minded their own business, had no interest in politics or war, this was unbelievable.

They had to leave. Children and adults cried, livestock bellowed, needing food. They began scurrying onto awaiting boats in Cerna-Voda on the Danube. The now homeless were resigned and devastated. Overcrowded vessels filled with disillusioned peoples heading for who knew where. They headed west, upstream on the Danube.

On the border with what was then Yugoslavia, a large German contingency welcomed the overtired travelers with promise of food and better times ahead. Though not very much convinced, they proceeded on the journey towards Austria. Not far from Vienna, the masses of people were made to leave the boat, directed to a large building, a *Lager*, where every family was given a room. The smaller families were to share with other families. It was here my brother Adi was born. It was cramped.

To this point, you've been hearing of what I had been told by my grandparents, parents, aunts and uncles. One of my father's cousins who had become a priest, "Pater Hannes," wrote a book describing in detail the people of the Dobrudja. After reading it, much of what I was told by my family fell into place.

I was about four years old at the time and it's here that I begin to remember things.

From here on in, I will tell the stories in the first person…

Chapter 1

War... The Journey Begins

It was 1941. I was the oldest of three children and remember crying much of the time, mostly because I was separated from my family, attending kindergarten. Every day we would wait in long lines for food distributions. The women worked in the kitchens doing laundry all day. The men worked on railroads repairing damaged tracks. The young men were ordered to the Eastern front.

People became hopeless, restless and demoralized. Many got sick of the overcrowding and poor diets. They wondered, what's next? We were promised evacuations to better housing in the country. We waited in anticipation. Slowly, some families were transferred out without knowing their exact destination. I remember hearing women crying all the time. Everything was just so sad. As a child you really can't understand. I just clung onto my mother's skirt not wanting to get lost in all this turmoil. How devastating this must have been for the adults – one can only imagine.

Finally, it was our turn to leave. Wherever we were headed had to be better than where we were leaving. The authorities said we would be sent to a farm. My father and grandfather were farmers. This was good news for us. We were put on a train – destination Prague, Czechoslovakia, we were told. "Oh my God, yet another country where we will once again be strangers," lamented my mother. If the situation wasn't bad enough, just outside Prague, she delivered her fourth child – a boy, Anthony. The baby was born near a military hospital. I don't remember where the rest of our family waited for them to return.

It was very cold in Prague and it was there I got my very first coat; dark green with grey rabbit's fur on the collar and cuffs. I remember this clearly as it was so different from any kind of clothing our family had before. Our family dressed mostly in black, the fashion of the old country. The women wore large woolen wraps with fringes – black, of course, or with white cotton lace for the unmarried girls. The men wore hats made of lamb's wool.

We headed off by train. How long exactly we were on that train, I really can't say, but for me, it was a very, very long time. At one stop we were transferred to a wagon and taken to a farming complex on the outskirts of a community named Bischkovitz. It was getting dark as we arrived. Someone ushered us inside a kitchen with the largest stove I'd ever seen. There were already some others in the kitchen standing around. At first, no one spoke, then, on cue everyone started crying. Words were no help. It was pointless. We could not understand each other's languages. My newborn baby brother Anthony started screaming and one of the women led us promptly upstairs to a room with three beds. We settled into the small room. We must have been exhausted – no one spoke.

Waking early the next morning – I'm not certain if either of my parents slept that night – we came downstairs together. The children were seldom left alone. We met even more people in the kitchen. One of the men who had been there yesterday spoke in broken German. He introduced the men and women and said to my father that they were the helpers or farmhands here. Father was to be the manager of this estate.

We all took a walk along this very large complex consisting of a good sized farmhouse, stables, barns, machinery, sheds, a large two-story grain storage, and a huge vegetable garden opposite a round driveway. All this property was encircled by a stone wall fastened by an immense iron gate. Outside the gate was a large fruit plantation with wide open fields beyond. To the left were several homes, these belonged to the workers. It was beautiful – yet no one ever smiled.

The native Czechs were friendly though we did not understand one another and communicated mostly by hand, by shrugs and nods. Everyone knew the workings of the farm and did their part. The children had the advantage of coming together from the start. We always found ways to play games; running, hiding, playing in the barns; none of this required a common language. When spring came we would join our folks in the field, in summer hayrides. And in the fall, we snuck into the barn, climbed up onto the beams and would jump. We also managed to get into trouble together. This beam jumping was one of those episodes that got us into trouble. Another was when we hid in the stables near the horses, playing hide and seek. This was prohibited and grandfather would become angry with us – his own grandchildren and the natives as well. We all understood a scolding.

It didn't take long for the kids to converse in Czech. Not perfect – but the Czech kids also picked up some German.

This proved to be a promising time for us – at least we children were happy. How our parents and grandparents felt, we didn't really know – their faces were always dour. I think though, in some way it was helpful to have children around.

On Sundays we drove to church in the neighboring town as ours did not have a Catholic church. This was the high point of the week. Father would hitch the two younger horses in front of the coach and we would ride through the country, with the "top down." Great fun! During the mass, the Czech people sang beautiful hymns. Many of the melodies were similar to our own. This, I felt, gave our parents some comfort. They loved singing.

At the harvest, my father was able to get some of our cousins from the *Lager* to come and help out. It was during that time he arranged for his sister, Monica and her family – which consisted of her husband Clemens and daughter, Maria – to stay with us. This was especially appreciated by our grandmother, who at that point seemed to be getting more sick and weak. These new members of our family were a gift to her. Tante Monica was her only daughter. We settled here comfortably and felt somewhat at ease. This happy reunion however, was short-lived.

We could hear thunder rolling in getting closer and closer. Then at times, it roiled further away. I suppose our parents did not want to worry us – it was, therefore "thunder." I must have been six years old at the time and remember not wanting to sleep alone when the thunder clapped. On top of this, I had to start school. I had to go away to a German boarding school in a town named Melnick. This was a nightmare – to leave family and friends and go so far away. I'm certain my parents had no other choice, and tried to calm my worries, telling me I would return to them at Christmas. This did nothing for me.

It was horrible at the boarding school. I don't think I learned a thing. I was forever crying, calling for my parents. Everyday day we had to stand in long lines for meals and every day we were lined up to be checked for lice. We slept in large overcrowded halls. I was heartbroken – not able to run home. I couldn't write yet what I felt. I had no one to talk to.

Finally it was Christmas break – which meant home. How I got home, I don't remember. I suppose someone picked me up. It was a blur. I just knew I was back home. I couldn't wait for my mother's cooking and baking. My mother had eight brothers and so had plenty of practice in the kitchen. Cooking and baking resonated throughout my life and this journal.

This homey feeling, however, did not last long. My father was commissioned to the Eastern front as a German soldier. How could this be? Everyone always said they only took the young men. What was to become of us? Of course, we had grandfather still, but he was old. Things started changing fast.

The bombings became more intense and frequent. No one knew what to do. The adults continued mechanically through their daily chores. The animals and the farm needed tending. We never heard from father. What we could hear about the war from the radio was dismal. One bright spot, if you can call it that, was that my mother kept me home from the boarding school. It was too dangerous.

Some of our cousins Anna, Matz, and my Onkel Florian – my mother's youngest brother – came to join us and to help out on the farm. Our Czech neighbors also pitched in. For the children, we were not so attuned to all that was going on with the war. The grownups tried to keep any bad news from us. Without much warning there was to be another baby brother – Alois.

In those days, women wore loose and roomy garments – not at all tight fitting. We did not know there was another brother on the way. He surprised us all. We were now five children – two girls and three boys. Little Alois made us all very happy. Named after my grandfather, he did not cry much. Not as much as Tony had – especially during the night. This was a bonus.

In April of 1945, one month after Alois was born, we had to quickly uproot and move. The war was coming to Bischkovitz.

There was a flurry of activity by the adults and we children were kept once again, in the dark; this time in a large middle room of the farmhouse. Grandmother read to us and prayed with us constantly. She carefully taught us the rosary.

One morning, very early, we were surprised to see from the kitchen window, three covered wagons standing outside on the circle drive. What excitement – we were going somewhere. The wagons were loaded with mostly food, water, feed for the horses and a large black kettle. We assumed we were going off on an adventure. Hoorah! But yet, more crying, embracing with the Czech workers and their children. Maybe this wasn't going to be the adventure I anticipated. All the kids joined in the chorus of tears. We waved miserably at the people we were leaving behind. Our little friends ran alongside the wagons, waving and calling until we turned the corner. Two of our wagons were pulled by horses and the third by oxen. Each of the main families had their own wagons. Grandfather led the wagons holding our family and two large work horses. Onkel Clemens followed with his family with the Sunday horses and one of the widows from our village took the wagon with the oxen to pull her wagon. Which direction we travelled, we had no idea, nor did we care. So long as our family was intact (minus of course, my father, who was still, as best we knew on the Eastern front and hopefully alive), that was all that mattered.

After several days we met up with a long caravan of wagons, just like ours. Heading westward, we tended to stick near the woods. Shots and explosions surrounded us and so open areas were avoided. The roads through the woods, though not very good, were much safer. Every so often someone's wagon would break down. The whole trek came to a halt until the wagon was put back in working order. At night, we would make camp, if possible near a stream or lake. We needed a spot for both horses and for us. It was frightening for us, hearing the shots ringing out through the evening. But there was something about our family's nearness that kept us calmed.

We avoided the villages where possible. This didn't always work out. The outskirts welcomed us more readily than perhaps the town folk who didn't know who we were or what we wanted or what we were up to. On one trip through a very small town, a group of men directed us to a warehouse where they made us all get out of the wagons and then took some of our belongings. Any items of value had been taken from us and then we were sent on our way. After repeated stops like these we avoided towns altogether. One small relief was they never harmed any of us.

One day, near a young tree farm, there was much shooting. We could hear people screaming and that alarming cry came closer and closer causing our caravan to come to a complete stop. We could see soldiers and civilians running and shooting each other. We were caught in the crossfire as they shot underneath our wagons from one ditch on one side of the road to the other. Mother made us lie on the very bottom of the wagon and be very still. I was terrified.

Finally, the fighting passed us, and the refugees all called out to see if anyone in our caravan had been hurt. We were lucky this time. Not even a horse or ox had been shot. We started up again and shortly after we passed an open field the women screamed out. The shocking sight displayed before us – all those bodies – like a field of bodies – some in uniform, some not. We ran out to the field to see if anyone was still alive. I held onto my mother's big skirt. My mother grabbed onto the little ones.

The bodies seemed to be covering the fields. Not a one looked to be alive. The women went around and closed their eyes while mumbling prayers. Weeping and lamenting constantly, that's what I heard. It was horrendous. The old men wanted to start burying the dead but the shooting could be heard nearing us again so everyone headed back to the wagons. The older men took charge, trying to comfort the hysterical women. The fighting continued and so did we. Not far down the road we came upon a broken down vehicle. Upon closer inspection, we found hard bread strewn all over a military truck. Some of the bread was stale and moldy. We all lunged for it anyway.

Grandmother called it a miracle.

On the next day, it was barely light. Grandfather and mother had just put the kettle on. Suddenly we heard above us, airplanes. Really, really close – they seemed on top of us. We hardly had time to jump off the wagons. These airplanes were diving and shooting at our wagons; just like you see in the movies – tat-tat-tat-tat. Everyone hit the ground as the next plane soared toward us spitting out bullets. It took about ten minutes or so and between the raining bullets, my grandfather went racing to the wagon to rescue Alois, our youngest brother, before the next attack.

That was so very close, for the wagon in front of us was now on fire. This was our Onkel Clemens' wagon. However, it was not completely destroyed and we were able to salvage it for use again with the help of the members of this wagon train. My new coat had been on that burning wagon as I had slept there the night before. The coat was no longer mine to wear. Other wagons in our caravan were not so lucky and were completely damaged, so the families were forced to double up in the remaining wagons.

Thankfully, none of us were harmed, however, one of our oxen had been struck and had to be put down. Grandfather and the other old men slaughtered it, once it was safe. We all had food once more and then we were on our way again. Just as we started up again, a large group of peasants came out of the woods carrying what appeared to be their belongings on their backs. No oxen, no horses, no wagons. They had nothing else. This group became part of ours. They mingled in with us trudging onward. Not really knowing where we were going but feeling somewhat safer in the company of others.

As we continued on, our wagon train was sometimes separated by explosions. Even more often, people would run up to our wagons with screaming children in their arms, asking if the child belonged to any of us. It was unbelievable. People wondered, "Where was God?"

It seemed we were going in circles. We had to avoid the danger zones which were everywhere. Thinking back on this, I can't believe our elders were able to cope and calm us every day. It doesn't seem real. My mother, alone with five little children, the baby only two months old, a dying mother-in-law, in the middle of nowhere. No food. No husband. Nothing.

On another evening we were making a rest stop, mostly for the horses. They just couldn't go anymore. Suddenly we heard girls screaming and running. One young woman came to our wagon and asked if she could take one of our little ones in her arms so that the Russian soldiers wouldn't take her. Mother let her hide in our wagon instead. We children all sat on top of her. Mother sat in the front of the wagon with Alois, the baby in her arm. If I could paint, I would try to capture this image.

Haunting.

This is how she sat when we traveled, I would sit next to her, then the rest of the kids, one by one and grandmother would be the end of the line. Grandfather always slept under the wagon. Shouting came closer and one of the soldiers shouted in our direction – "*Uhr, uhr davei!*" Onkel Clemens spoke some Russian and so he gave this soldier an alarm clock. The soldier became angry with this and threw it back in to the wagon. He was swaying, as if he was either hurt or drunk. At this moment, baby Alois began to cry. The soldier came closer to mother who was hunched over little Al. He mumbled something none of us could understand. It sounded as if he wanted to hush the child. He began humming a little melody and continued on.

It was another miracle, my grandmother said. Every time something went right, she would say this.

A day or so later we made camp with about half of the wagon train. The others fled in another direction. It was near a wide river or lake. I remember water. The horses were led to it straight away. It was getting dark. It was time for the children to go to sleep. Suddenly an explosion zipped through the dusk and everyone hit the dirt. Automatically, we all sprawled on the ground; arms clasping our heads. No one moved, not even the children cried. When no debris fell upon us, slowly people lifted their heads and stared in surprise. Yet again, and again we heard these explosions. Some said; "look across the water – they're exploding colorful bombs." No one could explain this. Bombs going off and no one getting hurt? Now thinking back on this, did this mark the end of the war? It was the summer of 1945. They were celebrating something. We actually had fun looking at this spectacle. Afterwards, the night became quiet once more.

The shooting became less frequent. Word got around that we were nearing the German border. The refugees, in their excitement pressed on, not bothering to stop to make their usual camp. It was dark, I remembered, traveling through the forest with trees protecting us. Then the border was in sight. Everyone who could walk ran to the guardrail separating us from Germany.

Tomorrow they would let us enter. The refugees seemed relieved. The adults came together and built a huge fire where we shared all of our last foodstuffs. It was a celebration, or so it seemed to us children. They even started singing. It started out with some melancholy tunes but then included folk songs that we children were able to join in. We thought, this is it – we're going home.

Grandmother told us the story of the prodigal son. She always included biblical references to any story she told. I thought the reason for this was because she was so near death during most of the journey. She was a petite woman, whereas my grandfather was a huge 'John Wayne" kind of man. Thinking back again, we would have never made it through without him. But what a match these two made.

The next morning started with much confusion and lamentation. We were not allowed across the border and were instead ordered away. It was unbelievable. Some of the refugees started arguing with these messengers and after shots rang out, we knew this was hopeless. A head count showed some of our members were missing. We assumed they had taken a chance at swimming across the river down where it was narrow. None of our extended family was among them. For that our elders were thankful.

A woman, who was among the refugees that had joined our caravan sometime midway through, pushed a baby buggy along with her screaming baby. Everything she owned was in the buggy. She refused to allow any of us to lift her burden into our wagons. I couldn't understand that – I still don't. However, as the wagon train turned around going east, the same woman passed us once again. The baby was no longer crying, but she was. Someone had found out, not that we children would have been informed of such tragedy, that her child had died. She did not want to bury this child in a strange place, but rather wished to bury the child on German soil. She vanished from our wagon train. I never knew what became of her.

Our people were losing hope of finding refuge anywhere. We were now out of food and money of course. The horses could graze on the side of the road. The refugees were not so fortunate. More than once, word got around that someone had been beaten or shot stealing from farmers – eggs, a chicken, a sack of flour.

When the authorities came around, we all stayed quiet. It was our fight for survival.

When I think back on this, about how people coped, I was a child who could see and hear but not really understand. Even now, I can't make sense of any of this.

We started traveling in circles once again. Another town and this time, during the search there was nothing to find. Our wagons were bare. So they looked over our group of refugees and demanded coats, blankets and boots. Any type of clothing we were wearing. My father's boots from way back in Rumania, which one of our lady friends wore. My grandfather's old shepherd coat – that also served as our cover at night. I never forgot that coat. It was long, with dark lamb's wool inside with worn grayish leather on the outside. It had shiny spots on the elbows and back but was the warmest cover ever.

These items they took from us.

After more aimless wandering, we were led to a very large complex or cooperative. It had a huge gate with a wall around it. Inside was a circular drive – to the right was where they unloaded us. Our horses and wagons were taken away and we were ushered into a barren building. No furniture. We just sat on the floor. Each family got a corner of the room to settle in. More turmoil, more crying. People resigned themselves, waiting on the floor for what would come next.

A group of people came in, looked us over and began sorting the old men into one group, the women in another and finally, the children and the sick in yet another group. Some women brought food which nearly caused a riot. It felt really wonderful getting a full meal. Someone gave directions to where all the different groups would be working. Grandfather and our uncle would be working in the group tending to the cattle and pigs. Mother and my Tante Monica were sent to milking detail – every morning and every evening. Grandmother and the rest of the elderly and sickly had to take care of the children.

Still, it was a better existence than being shot at or wandering with no place to go. We had a roof over our heads and we felt safe. There were many children in our barren hall. After a few days of getting to know one another, we wanted to get out of doors to explore. I was the youngest of this bunch. While the little ones were napping, the elders were busy with the babies and only after much nagging, we were allowed to go. The older kids spoke Czech and assured them they would take care of the younger kids like me.

This was a huge property we had been taken to. Beyond the circular drive there was a huge fancy house. Thinking back, I never recalled seeing anyone coming or going from this house. The house was surrounded by a beautiful garden with a high fence. We could not go there. That we knew. There were so many other outbuildings and barns to explore. What an exhilarating feeling. Away from those cooped up wagons and the barren room. We were free. Large orchards and fields of vegetables and wheat, mixed with huge areas of beautiful wild flowers spread out for as far as you could see – all for us to enjoy.

We would race through the fields laughing and falling and getting up and falling yet again. On one such race we heard the pigs making a lot of noise, and having grown up on the farm, this meant feeding time. We weren't allowed inside any of the barns or stables as this would disturb the animals. The girls, as usual, minded this rule. The boys however, peeked through the open door and saw the farmhand filling a large container with steaming potatoes. As he went for more, the boys ran in and grabbed some of the potatoes, darting out as fast as they had in. We all sat against the outside wall of the barn. We all got a piece of hot potato. The girls first protested – it would be wrong – but we quickly gave in, indulging in this wonderful meal.

If my grandmother had ever found out she would have quickly proclaimed we would all be going straight to hell.

When we got home we had some milk that my mother had brought from the stables. She did this every day, bringing a bucketful for all the children.

One day, we children were standing in the hallway scheming our next adventure. (I don't know why we were not ordered to go to school. It was early summer – too early for summer break. I'm certain it was still in session. Maybe they didn't want us to mix with the natives out of some fear we might start something. I never was able to figure that one out.) We suddenly heard trucks coming closer. The gates opened and two military trucks entered the estate. We all hid inside waiting to see what would happen next. Soldiers with rifles jumped out. One opened the back and more soldiers spilled out. A command was barked out and the soldiers made one line and marched together to the back by the fields. That morning the children stayed inside. The elders ordered us away from the windows.

The soldiers returned later about noon, sat down and began to eat food out of cans. Some of the soldiers stood up eating some sort of orange fruit. They threw the peels behind them which landed on the grass inside the circle drive. We slowly made our way downstairs to the doorway. The boys dared each other to go run and see what the soldiers had thrown away. I'm certain these armed soldiers saw us, but they continued their lunch and kept an eye on us.

One of the boys ran to the grassy circle and grabbed some of the orange stuff and ran back to us. We tasted it and soon everyone wanted some. The other boys decided they would get more. All of a sudden, orange peels were flying at us. We became more daring. We all fetched some and ran inside. It was delicious – these orange peels. At about this same time the soldiers rose and marched back into the fields.

That evening when our elders returned, they told us the American soldiers had transported German prisoners of war here to work. The women were excited. Maybe these soldiers would know the whereabouts of their husbands, brothers or sons. But who would have the courage to ask?

The next morning we were already waiting for the army trucks. They waved at us and we returned the greeting. At lunchtime we eagerly awaited the soldiers coming to their lunch spot but nothing happened. One of the American guards said something and waved us to come over. No one moved. One of the prisoners called in German – it was alright – we would not be hurt. Slowly, we brushed alongside the wall of the building. No one wanted to be the first. We stopped – not quite certain of the situation. All at once, as if in unison, they stretched out their hands with oranges and chocolate. We all recognized chocolate bars, what child doesn't. We inched closer still.

I still get emotional whenever I think of that moment – the victors, the defeated and the innocents all coming together.

From then on, we, the children, would anxiously await the American military trucks. Our caution had vanished. We were no longer afraid of soldiers, even those carrying rifles. We felt we were now friends and things would surely get better.

In the following days, some of the elders inquired again if the soldiers had heard or served with their missing loved ones and exchanged information on them. Sure enough, some of them recognized the names and indicated there were some men with those names somewhere in the camp. They would try and bring these prisoners to them the following days.

The reunions, as you would guess, were loud, happy and emotional. We actually saw people smiling and hugging and talking excitedly. This we had not experienced in too long a time. The children hung in the background taking it all in.

Some of the named prisoners were wounded they said and could not come until later. The women persevered awaiting their individual reunions. What they lacked in material possessions was overflowing in their need to see their war weary loved ones.

Not long after – it could have been days or weeks – we were informed that our stay here had come to an end. We would be transferred to another location. That was all the information we were given. We wondered if this next stop would be better or worse. We children didn't worry that much – we had each other and the bombing and shooting had seemed to come to a halt. Before we got our orders, the troops had to move on. Their long convoys passed the compound as we children stood on either side of those great doors, waving good-byes. Sadly, we felt they were abandoning us.

Our cousin Maria, at the very moment, gave us a quick English lesson and we all shouted, "Farewell." The soldiers smiled and waved back. Some even shouted, "Auf Wiedersehen."

The next morning mother and Tante Monica came back from milking armed with buckets of milk and loaves of bread. It was a feast. They rationed it all. It had to last us for some time. How long exactly, we didn't know, but we had to be prepared.

When it came time to leave, we received some bad news. We were not to get our horses back for the next leg of our journey. Grandfather, especially was heartbroken. These horses were part of his life. Instead, trucks arrived and the refugees were all piled on top of each other; much too close for comfort. Everyone seemed to be going through the motions, as if in some sort of trance. We had no idea where we were going and no one seemed to care. Over bumpy roads we were taken to a train station in Pilsen. A train awaited us.

A group of officials came, looked us over and then divided so many people per car. We held on to each other. Many started crying. All the old men had to line up and follow the officials to the front car of the long train. This train, without any windows, scared us – it looked like a freight train they were trying to get us to board. The women began screaming, and grasping on tight to their men folk. This ordeal had been painful enough – not to be separated from loved ones.

The children clung to their parents, refusing to let go. I always thought our family was so tough. My mother seldom cried. She was always the one calming us. She held baby Al in one arm and Adi, four years old at that time, in the other. Tante Monica carried Anthony, three years old. My sister Pat (Perpetua) and I held fast to my mother's big black skirt. Maria, our cousin carried the few items we had left. We were loaded into the cars toward the back – what seemed like miles from the men. We were all shoved inside. Not only was the train missing windows, we discovered as we entered, there was not a roof on the rail cars either!

The first people inside took refuge in the corners, marking their areas with the few belongings they carried. The rest of us were resigned to whatever space was left available. The doors closed and were locked from the outside. Children cried themselves to sleep; women stared with worn, reddened eyes, leaning up against the walls of the train, paralyzed to that one spot.

The train took off, but exactly where or in what general direction, we had no clue. It was dusk. We couldn't judge by the sun, or the moon for that matter. No trees or towers to mark a position. Everything was inky black.

In the morning children began clamoring for something to eat. Bread and cold potatoes were produced. Cold or not, it was food. Mother was nursing the baby. I never saw her eat and was surprised as she stayed so very strong without eating. I'm certain it was for our benefit she kept this strength.

We travelled for some time without stopping. The children used a pot propped in a corner to go to the bathroom. Suddenly, the train came to a screeching halt. People fell on top of each other. A convoy came alongside us. We could hear men whooping and shouting – their language sounded like that of the American soldiers. We all sat very still. All of a sudden, like hail, choco-late, crackers, cookies, cigarettes, gum and some small cans came pouring into our car. These packages looked like rations for soldiers. It was like Christmas. How did these soldiers know we were in here? We assumed they were soldiers, perhaps making their way to a rendezvous point.

Another miracle – so said my grandmother.

Someone from the outside shouted we could go no further. The tracks ahead had been damaged and the time for repairs was unknown. More unhappy chatter. The doors opened. All we could see around us was a sea of destruction. Piles of stones, bricks, rubble and twisted iron, were everywhere. Not a single building was standing for as far as we could see. No one made a sound – not even a gasp. I think shock overtook us all. There were no people in sight. The women stayed put. They did not want to disembark. It looked like the end of the world.

Grandmother pulled us closer to her and started praying the rosary. At the time, I could not believe this praying could change what we saw.

Slowly people climbed down the ramps. Others jumped down. We looked around. There were the old men coming toward us from the front of the train – searching. There were great hugs but also cries as this reunion played out in this decimated landscape. Someone said we were in Nüremberg. The tracks would not be ready until morning. Food would be distributed. We would be on our own until the train was ready to depart.

Although we were happy to be outside to stretch our limbs, most stayed near the train. There was really no good place in sight. No tree or bush, or piece of wood or grass to perhaps sit. The debris came right up to the tracks. How the train was able to get to even this point is something I still can't comprehend. Some Red Cross nurses came by with a cart filled with water, food and first aid. We really didn't suffer too many injuries. Exhaustion was our biggest ailment and we leaned on each other as medicine.

Some of the children became curious and began to climb these mounds of stone and rubble. The elders quickly snatched their children for fear these piles of rubble might yet contain unexploded bombs. Those children that were beyond their parent's reach quickly scrambled back – diligently obeying this command.

It started to drizzle. The men went off in search of some sort of shelter. My grandfather and Onkel Clemens came back to fetch us. They had found remnants of a collapsed staircase that could protect us for the night. It was dangerous, navigating through this obstacle course. Grandmother was so weak at this point so grandfather carried her to our makeshift shelter. Baby Al, Tony and Adi didn't look so good either. The environment was toxic. It seemed that somehow, our parents were able to make some order out of this chaos. We children just wanted an arm around us and something to eat – we were always hungry.

Early the next morning we heard the train whistles and rushed back as fast as we could. I often wondered as I got older, why all of us returned to this train? Did they all return? They must have for I recognized the faces that had been pressed together in our car. Why wouldn't some try to escape into the fields or the woods? There must have been something alive out there beyond these mounds of destruction. Was it the hopelessness or fear of the unknown? Was it a greater risk running away, or staying on this wretched freight train?

24

The families were again separated – not willingly, but there was no other choice given. It seems that more people became noticeably sick. The travelers tried to keep as much distance as they could from each other. Some appeared near dead – coughing and gasping for air. Our grandmother was among them. She was weak and feverish. She would wail out loud the names of her missing sons, my father Mathias and his older brother Rafael. She also began urgently naming off her ten brothers and sisters, who like us, were somewhere roaming around Europe. No defined destination in sight. Without any means of communication. We had no idea where they were just as they had no idea where we might be. When my grandmother came out of her delirium, she would pray incessantly.

Most people seemed to have given up hope at this point. They drifted in silence. Another stop and we were shuttled into a large stone fortress. This town was called Ansbach. Here we were ordered to line up in rows and rows and asked to give identifying information. This had been asked from us time and time again. We were well rehearsed on our responses. We were then given food and some blankets.

Families were grouped together and told to wait further instruction. It was August 15, 1945. Trucks lined up and our travel weary people filled them. These trucks were partially opened, with tarps pulled back. This was far better than our previous mode of transportation. The trucks took us through a most serene countryside, seemingly untouched by the rages of war.

Chapter 2

The Village

We arrived at a village named Wettringen, near Rothenburg ob der Tauber. In the middle of this village was the market square. Here we stopped and the back of the truck opened. Villagers came to the truck to pick up those refugees that would stay in their homes for some time. Others came just to look at these new curiosities. Some of the villagers smiled, others did not.

Our family was the last off the truck. We were also the last picked. Perhaps it was the number of us? Maybe they couldn't find a shelter large enough to accommodate our whole family? I remember it was almost evening as the cows were just being brought to the trough. This trough was in the square, just in front of where we were standing.

Just then, from a large farm house/inn across the square, a woman started waving at us bidding us to come forward. Several children were milling around her. Her name was Frau Moenikheim. They cleared an area at the inn that spanned the entire width of the second floor of a building and had previously been used as a dancehall for the village.

Tables and benches were placed just so, in order for us to have enough room to spread out. The daughters of the house brought so much food. Hallelujah! Then they brought blankets and mats for us to rest on. We slept well that night. Maybe the best sleep ever. We were most thankful to these generous people. Tante Monika and her family were placed in a room adjacent to us. In a few days, they told us two rooms would be finished for us on the third floor – a kitchen and a bedroom. Incredible!

The following day, we had to register in order to obtain welfare. Until our people could get work, we needed it. This must have been crushing for these once land-rich farmers, to have to take handouts and work for others. They soon found work however. They were able bodied and the harvest was near. The natives were all too happy for the extra help.

Within the first week of our arrival however, my brother Adi had to be sent to a health sanitarium in the Black Forest. He had been undernourished and seemed to have suffered the most. I don't remember how long he was gone – it could have been several weeks, or several months. There was so much going on in such a very short period of time. He was only four years old yet he never fussed about it. Brave little boy.

The harshness of our flight was catching up with us. My mother and baby Al were suffering under a fever and chills that lasted for quite a while. The doctor called it jaundice. Grandmother often told us later, at the time they did not think Al would make it since he was only six months old at the time. They both however, survived. They were tough.

As we began to settle in, we children found much to explore. Meeting the town's children was at first a bit difficult. Although we spoke German, it was a different dialect and so sometimes we had difficulty understanding one another. This was soon remedied. We were off playing, getting to know the children of

Wettringen. We were also anxiously waiting for the school year to start.

My sister Perpetua and I were registered into the first and second grade respectively. The last time I had been in school was that wretched boarding school in Czechoslovakia. What a difference. I loved this school and the teachers. I couldn't wait to go to class every morning. Adi, who had just recently returned from the Black Forest, was enrolled into kindergarten with his younger brother Tony. The kindergarten was run by Sister Emma. Sister Lina was the village nurse. We got to know each of them very well. Sister Emma and Sister Lina lived near the church. But then again, everyone lived near the church. The school was next to the cemetery beside the church. In front of the wall that surrounded this complex was a row of tall Linden trees. Alongside these trees ran a humble spring that was the beginning of the river Tauber. This spring began just outside the village and ran right through it. Every spring the Tauber would overflow, flooding sections of the village. One spring old Herr Strecker fell into the Tauber and was saved just before he would have been sucked into the drainpipe. It was the local children that pulled him out. One of the boys yelled, "Look! Herr Strecker is learning to swim!" which got their attention, thankfully.

Shortly after the school year began we had quite a shock. It wasn't a school day, because we were all upstairs at the Moenikheim's house. All of a sudden, our kitchen door opened and there was our father – returned from the war. What a commotion. Everyone poured into that third floor combination living room/bedroom/kitchen. We all piled in to grab hold of our father, "Matz" as the adults called him. We were happy to see him of course, but for some odd reason, my brothers held back a little. Perhaps they didn't remember him? Didn't recognize him? He had never seen baby Alois before, Al had been born while father was away. A few days after his arrival, Tony, then age three asked my mother when that man was going to leave again!

My father had been a prisoner of war and had been held near Dresden. It would take him years and years to tell us of his horrendous and complicated experiences at that camp. When the camp had been liberated he spent time working on a vast farm while desperately trying to locate us, his family. He inquired if anyone knew the names of Bachmeier, Ruscheinsky or Mueller in the hopes of finding a connection to us. After several months he found us through the Red Cross and through relatives who had been transplanted in and around Regensburg.

Soon after our father's arrival, we moved into a larger dwelling on the first floor of the coach house toward the back of the main house. It was bigger than what we were used to. The upstairs apartment was occupied by the local policeman and his family. It felt good and safe here. The village was finally our home.

The town itself was charming and picturesque. Something you would see out of a children's storybook. It was kept meticulously clean. There seemed to be an unwritten competition for who had the most attractive, homes, stable, barn. The women competed for the most lush gardens and colorful window boxes.

Every Saturday, the young people would sweep the street in front of their unpaved property, first sprinkling it not to make too much dust. On Sunday morning, all the adult villagers would go to church dressed in their Sunday best. In the afternoon, the young ones would go to Sunday school. It was all very orderly; their parents would be pleased and the neighbors would not complain. The village was very small, you see, and if the parents heard anything unflattering from anyone in the village, you would get into big trouble. This was probably a good thing. Nothing really got out of hand although the young people really didn't appreciate the idea much, just like everywhere else in the world.

Not only were we foreigners, we were also Catholic. We discovered the locals were mostly of the Protestant faith. The townspeople and especially the teachers never treated us any differently even though we were one of the few Catholics in the town. At one point a priest came on his motorcycle to teach the Catholic refugees. The village elders arranged for us to have mass in their church every other Sunday. It was a generous gesture and became part of our bi-weekly ritual.

A second policeman was hired for the village which meant our family had to vacate the coach house. This time we were settled into another farm house – just across the street from the church and kitty corner from the school. Blacksmiths on both sides of us. What excitement!

The couple that owned the farm house, Herr and Frau Strecker, was childless and retired. Their barn was leased out to other farmers but the premises remained intact. We were to live on the first floor, which pleased our parents having five children running around. The grandparents would have a bedroom upstairs. We had a large kitchen with an old stove, an open chimney, a table with two long benches from our first landlord and one trunk. Next to the kitchen was a pantry with a clay floor and plain shelves with the tiniest window and a screen. I had never seen a window with a screen before.

There was no running water – for that we had to go to the village pump. To the right of the kitchen was a small bedroom, and next to that was the large room called *die gute Stube*. Since we were so many children, this room served as the bedroom for the five of us and our parents slept in the little bedroom which also served as our living room. It was more economical heating up this little room in winter. In the evening, the door was left open in order to warm our room. Mom or my grandmother would put a hot brick wrapped in a towel and rub the beds before we went to bed.

Our furniture was mostly donated to us by the locals. After sometime there, we actually got something new, two single beds, one for my sister and one for me. We felt rich – my sister and I.

Our father now had a regular job as a forest worker. It was not what he had hoped to be doing – after all he was a farmer, but he would have regular work and this was important especially in a farming community where the best jobs were seasonal. We did not think of ourselves as being poor. There are poor and there are poor. We did not count ourselves among the latter.

Our family got a small piece of land outside the village where we could grow our own vegetables. This was most helpful. Grandfather raised rabbits to supplement our food supply. After school we would go along the roads outside the village, digging up dandelions for these rabbits. This was fun and carefree – and didn't at all seem like a chore. Our parents allowed us to be happy – they didn't want to burden us with unnecessary worries. We had experienced enough *angst* to last us a lifetime.

I liked school very much. We had wonderful teachers. The lower grades, first, second and third were in one classroom. Fräulein Meisner was the teacher who came from Rothenburg – her hometown. She lived in one room next to the stairs in the school building. Fourth, fifth and sixth were in another room. The teacher was Herr Strehl. Seventh and Eighth grade were very special. These were run by *Hauptlehrer* Herr Oechsner.

We started every morning with a song. Our classroom was across the street from the blacksmith so the first thing our teacher requested was that we open all the windows and sing so as to drown out the blacksmiths' hammers. What a challenge – each kid wanted to outdo the next. Although some sang a little off key – that did not hold back the rest of the singers. It was inspiring. Most of my musical repertoire began here and ended up keeping me focused throughout some of my more troubling teenage years.

Herr Oechsner was also the organist. At service on Sunday mornings we could hear the organ and the congregation clear through the walls of our home. He had such a presence in our community. He was awesome.

When someone died, it resembled an old foreign movie or maybe something from *The Godfather*. All the town people attended and wore their Sunday best which was always black. The school children would lead the procession to the *Friedhof*, or cemetery. We sang somber hymns as we marched along. To my mind, it was a most beautiful tradition.

As mentioned earlier, every second Sunday, Father Franz Schroeder would come to this diaspora and say mass for ten Catholic families. He would park his motorcycle in our courtyard. We kept the suitcase at our home that held his vestments. Why us? Well, it seemed we had everything needed for the services. My father and grandfather always were the ushers. My brothers were the altar boys. Mother would take good care of the altar linens and we all had strong voices and could sing well. This was part of our heritage. Not professional. There was no money or opportunity for that but just about all of our relatives could sing really well. We had to sing all our songs a cappella – for we had no organist. This however, did not hold us back.

On the major holidays we would walk to the parish church in Bellershausen. This was a neighboring village about five kilometers from Wettringen. On special holidays, like the feast of Corpus Christi and Pfingsten, we would take the train to Schillingsfürst – which was about eight kilometers from our home. They had a large Catholic church there – very beautiful.

This was always a most exciting occasion for us youngsters – not that we were overly religious, like our grandmother – rather all that excitement came from the massive festival processions. This left a lasting impression on me. The brass bands were the best. They were powerful and led the faithful in some of the most beautiful hymns as they marched through the town. All the little ones wanted to march alongside them.

On the feast of Corpus Christi, the buildings along the way were decked out in flowers, greenery and colorful banners. Even the ecumenical differences were acknowledged. The first outdoor altar was traditionally placed in front of the Protestant rectory even though Corpus Christi was a Catholic holiday. This was unusual; however it seemed that they also wanted to acknowledge our faith and celebration. The ladies decorated this altar with the most brilliant peonies in town. The second altar was uphill and the music became somewhat weaker – though not much. This particular altar as well as the third and fourth were sponsored by the various Catholic villagers who lived around the area. The third altar was placed in front of the Institute for Catholic Girls. Of course, here, the young ladies and all the assigned nuns sang beautifully. My sister, Perpetua, would later become a student there.

The fourth altar was inside the castle courtyard. Here the brass band pulled out all the stops. They led the worshipers in one of my favorite hymns *"Ein Haus voll Glorie schauet weit uber alle Land."* It was awesome. The echo bounced off the castle walls. The children were startled by the massive sound of it. The first time I heard it, I thought "the next stop must be heaven's gate" – then again, I was a child – maybe seven years old.

No one in Wettringen worked on Sundays. After services and lunch, which was the main meal, the youngsters were free to roam the countryside. Wettringen as I mentioned before, was a tiny village clustered around the market square. Immediately surrounding it were wide meadows and fields. The landscape then turned into sloping hills covered by dense forests. Springtime was the best. Everything was green and the cherry, plum and apple trees were in full bloom. Wildflowers covered the meadows and we could not wait to race up the hills and either roll or run down.

There was one particularly challenging and very steep path up into the woods. The children from the neighboring village called Grüb used it every day to come to school. It was a winding path with partially exposed tree roots that provided uneven stairs. We would dare one another to run down this obstacle course – to see who could do it the fastest without falling. This was thrilling.

We also explored the woods for the first berry patches. When the time was right we wanted to be the first ones there. I don't remember our parents ever worrying about us being outdoors during these countryside explorations. Probably because we played mostly in groups and we stayed away from the "danger" zones – those that were *verboten*. The only thing we really needed to watch out for was that our shoes were clean before we entered the house. We didn't have two or three pair of shoes. We only had the one pair, and since the next day was a school day, we had to make certain our shoes were the shiniest – my grandmother insisted.

Our brothers played soccer like all the other kids. They played wherever they could – on the market square, in the streets, in the rain, in the mud. Whenever someone had a ball – out they would go to play. No one had cleats at that time. Father would be furious if the boys had either wet or banged up shoes after playing soccer all day. Grandmother would calm him down. She would stuff their high top shoes with pieces of crumpled paper or cloth and then place them next to our potbelly stove to dry. Early the next morning she would spit shine them before any of us even awakened. We asked her why she did this. She replied, "Well, I really can't do much else anymore."

Once we got to the upper classes, from sixth, seventh grade and up, we no longer had as much free time. The farmer's children had to help out in the fields and that included us. The lady of the house would reward us with a basket of whatever we were harvesting in exchange for our help. Most farmers had machines to mow the fields, some had tractors and some still used horses. They needed as many hands as possible to turn the hay. This had to be done three times – until the hay was totally dry. Everything was raked into clean rows and the fastest person would take the lead while the rest would scramble to keep up.

In the beginning your arms would ache and blisters were common. Soon, however, you got used to it. The best part was the vesper – when food was brought out to the fields. It was like a picnic. The farmer's daughters would bring sandwiches and *Most* – apple wine, the local specialty, for the adults and water for the kids. We would all head for shade under the nearest tree and dig in.

When the hay was dried, the horses were hitched to the wagon and the men would reach up with a pitchfork to a person standing on top of the wagon casting up dry hay. The load had to be just so – you couldn't have a lopsided load. The sons had to make sure of it, so as not to tip over on the bumpy roads home. They would never hear the end of it from the man of the house if it wasn't done properly. We also had homework to do and this had to be done before it got dark so as not to waste electricity. It was a hectic time.

Our summer break did not begin until the end of July which also marked the end of the haymaking season and a well-deserved break. Most of the villages would celebrate their *Kirchweih Fest* – the feast of the local patron saint. A carousel, large swings and an ice cream stand would all be set up in the market square. A lively band would play in the dancehall and the children from the neighboring villages would come and mingle with the locals. We were not yet old enough to join on the dance floor, so we would squeeze along the hallway window to watch the dancers and revelers.

This was a great opportunity to get rumors going – particularly if someone was dancing more than once with the same boy or girl. We couldn't wait until we were old enough to join in this merry making. However, since that wouldn't be happening for quite some time we would have to find other amusements – which took us to the carousel and the swings. But we liked watching all the grown-up activity the best.

Our family's garden plot just outside the village was one of our favorites. We could sit or lay on the grass with a book. You could hear the water splashing over the stones from a brook nearby. Sometimes you would just stare at the sky overhead, watching the clouds change and dream of faraway places. All of a sudden you would come out of your peaceful daydream, often by a frog leaping out into your space.

Early in the spring, it was shearing time and the local shepherd would blow his whistle in the market square which would bring the sheep running in from the outlying meadows. In the evening they would be corralled in by their respective owners. Before the shearing began, the sheep were thrown into a small nearby lake to get their first scrubbing. This happened over and over – catching sheep and throwing them into the lake. It was always great excitement, watching the struggling of the sheep not wanting to go into the lake and the owners and their children wrestling the sheep to get them back in.

The women did most of the shearing as the men had the job of holding the sheep tight as the process went on. It was a spectacle. Before they could make yarn out of the wool it had to be washed and combed repeatedly with two metal brushes. Then finally, it would be ready for the women to use on their spinning wheels. I can still remember my grandmother spinning away behind hers and her hands would get really oily. We were also involved in this production by holding out our arms so that the yarn could be strung between them into skeins and then into balls. There was usually enough yarn to keep the women busy all winter – knitting socks, mittens, sweaters, leggings, scarves. The only bad thing about these homemade woolens was how many washes and wearings it took to make the itching go away.

In September, just about when school started, the grain harvest would be upon us. This brought even more hard work. Our area grew mostly wheat, rye, oats, potatoes and beets. The farmers would bring back their bounty to the thresher. Your skin always had nasty scratches during this season. You had to wear long sleeves and long skirts or pants and hats or scarves to protect yourself from the wheat and the scorching sun. Every procedure had to be performed so that the final stacks were placed in perfect rows before they were brought back to the barns for threshing. This was really hard and you felt it mostly stinging your eyes and lungs. At this point, you were actually looking forward to school.

Next the potatoes were ready to be harvested as were the apples and pears. On weekends during this season, the mayor of the town would announce the annual auction. Many would come out to put a bid on the harvest of one tree. Most people had picked their favorite tree along the parkways way in advance. The bidding would therefore become quite fierce. The winning *Hausfrauen* would take these apples and produce applesauce, strudels, and dried apples which were placed on large screens and then stored in the attic to be eaten later.

The *Fallobst* – apples that fell on the grass, would be made into apple cider. This was intoxicating. The sweet smell coming from the presses attracted not only the villagers but also many bees. You always had to be careful when getting too near the presses. The farmers would always generously allow the kids to sample the ciders. You could only have so much – too much and you ended up in the outhouse for long periods of time.

The bulk of the cider would be placed into large barrels that would be rolled into the cellar for fermentation. *Most* was the name of the end product and was by far the most popular local drink. It was at this point it became an adults-only beverage – too much alcohol for the kids.

Back in school, our teacher would take us on field trips which were most informative. Most of these trips were in the vicinity where we could walk to, like the forest or a particular meadow where we could learn about rare flowers and trees. Some of these specimens were protected by laws and could not be picked or disturbed. The next day we would have to write an essay so you had to pay attention all the time.

On one of these outings, we took our bikes as the trip would last all day. This one involved the geographic and natural resources of our neighboring communities. We had to recognize all of the villages from afar, by their church steeples or famous gate. We had to name the river that ran near the town, what products were produced there, the population, etc. Before we left the schoolyard that day, Herr Oechsner stated he would take the lead and that *"Mueller"* – that was me, would bring up the rear.

"Oh, no," – I probably had the worst bicycle. Each part had come from someone else's old bike. I was not particularly fond of riding it. If this wasn't bad enough – I was also to provide a running commentary as we rode. I couldn't refuse. As you might guess, everything went just fine – regardless of my fears beforehand. By late afternoon, we rode, but many times walked our

bikes up the side of hill. On our left was the forest, and to the right, sloping meadows stretching all the way to the next farming community. As I was explaining the scenery, I got too near the gravel that lined the road and lost my balance. As I fell, I landed on a lone hiker, walking in the same direction.

I was upset and apologetic as we both got up. All my classmates had gathered and as my teacher hurried back, the old man brushed off his clothes, smiled at me and assured me he was not hurt. What a relief. The boys put my chain back on and off we went. Of course, I never heard the end of that embarrassing situation and the boys continued laughing at me long after. My teacher however, never brought the incident up again. My father prohibited me from using the bike for a long time after.

Soon, the task of preserving for the winters was upon us. Cabbage to sourkraut was a major undertaking. Large baskets full of these heads would get shredded on slicing boards then put in good sized stone tubs and punched down with salt. This was covered with a round, clean wooden lid that would nestle in a fitted ring. A heavy, super scrubbed stone would be anchored on top of the lid and then this concoction would be stored in the cellar.

Another huge event after the harvest but before winter was the slaughtering of a pig for the families to consume. This was to last us the entire winter. Depending on the size of the farm – maybe two would be slaughtered. All hands were on deck. Most of us young ones ran away at the gory sight. However, once the sausage making started – we were back. Most of the meat would be salted and put in large containers for a few days. It would then be hung in the open chimney, which every house had, to smoke. The end product was *Schinken* – smoked ham, a famous delicacy.

The *Hausfrau* would prepare the broth – plentiful after

preparing the meats and sausages. Whichever household was slaughtering the pig would produce this delicious broth for the town. People would scoop up bucketsful. This broth, coupled with farina dumplings or noodles, was absolutely delicious – Yum.

At the onset of winter another chore required gathering wood from the forests to build fence posts, and to obtain necessary fire wood. Although coals were also used, many stoves and hearths were fired with wood. This was done almost as an art form. My grandfather was just such an artist. Grandfather chopped wood all the time into smaller logs. He built several cupolas of firewood that would last us through the entire winter and beyond.

Our father and his fellow forest workers had an especially hard time during the winter. There was no transportation to and from the forest and the dirt roads right after the war were in such bad repair due to all the heavy wagons using the roads during the harvest. He would bundle himself so that only his eyes and eyebrows showed and these brows were frozen like icicles when he got home. The good thing about his job was that we always got the most perfect *Tannenbaum*.

For me, I thought winter was the best season of the year and this particular year was no exception. This would conclude my primary education at the old school house. Our teacher, Herr Oechsner, made a continuous effort to make this last year stand out in our memories. He seemed to want to prepare us for that big world out there. I would marvel at this time, thinking, why do we need to know all of this history – why these historical events – why the terribly difficult math problems – how about those really long poems. None of this made sense at the time. As I grew older, I would catch myself at times and smile…."so that's what Herr Oechsner meant by that….."

His introduction to us of the classics was most memorable. He played the violin and on that last Advent, he invited the other teacher's wife – Frau Moritz – a soprano, to sing for us. It was the first time in my life I had experienced such a recital. The one solo that stood out, and still does, is Franz Schubert's *Wiegenlied – Mille Cherubini in coro*. Herr Oechsner accompanied her soothing voice with his tender violin which brought forth a completely different perspective on this man – my teacher. Before I had only perceived him as a burly, strict but just man. After this performance, our annual school nativity presentation seemed so simple and plain even though I got to play Mary with a singing part.

On Christmas Eve day, the men got off work early. Grandfather and the older siblings ran out to meet father coming from the forest. He let us help him carry this most beautiful *Tannenbaum* home. We would bring this tree first to the barn to let the boughs drop. There was no decorating the tree as the *Tannenbaum* would be dressed "magically" while we were all at midnight mass. Nobody questioned this as all the other children in the village experienced the trimming of the tree in the same manner. Not until you were older – perhaps with a family of your own – were you in on this secret.

We always had lots of snow as I recall. We anxiously awaited our long pilgrimage to midnight mass in the neighboring village – well more realistically three villages away – of Bellershausen. Only the men and the older children could take this journey. It was five kilometers away and cross country – in deep snow – and most of the time the roads were hardly passable. We would start out shortly after supper. Onkel Alois and our cousins would gather at our house and after we were fully bundled up wearing everything we owned, we headed out. The men led the way to block out the harsh wind and the children would follow in their footsteps, close behind. This was almost impossible. We would need to take two steps for every single step of theirs.

The landscape was not even. Over rows of plowed fields,

then sometimes uphill, then over a frozen creek, it was treacherous. The air was so clear however, I can't remember ever having to fight through a storm on Christmas Eve. After the shortest of rests, someone would start singing and we would all chime in. We knew so many Christmas songs; we never had to repeat any even on the way home. As we neared the first village everyone became very quiet. We peeked into the windows of the village houses, admiring the sparkling Christmas trees. I felt like shouting.

Over the train tracks and we were halfway there. It was nighttime, certainly, but it was never pitch dark as you could always see with the stars lighting up the night. There was still another frozen brook we had to cross. This one had rows of poplar and willow trees growing alongside. The willows looked so scary against the starlit sky. It reminded me of a powerful poem we had learned – *Der Erlkönig*. I'm pretty certain it was Goethe's poem. I would grab the hand of the person next to me and I would soon become calm again.

In the distance we could hear bells ringing. Soon we could see the steeple of the little church peeking out over the little hill. As we crested the hill, the town opened up in front of us, and there was the church and its familiar steeple. We knew we were just in time.

The organ music welcomed us in. Once inside we would separate into our designated areas – the women on the left, the men on the right and the children in front also separated – boys on the right, girls on the left. It took the duration of the mass to get warm and after the final *Stille Nacht* we were once again off into the wintery wonderland. The way home always seemed shorter – anticipating all the goodies back at home.

Our *Tannenbaum* was fully trimmed when we arrived at home and we could smell a mixed scent of smoked sausages and

Streuselkuchen. Food for us was the most important, even over-taking gifts under the tree. We were no longer cold. Mother had set out every single food item we had in the house – Oranges-one each-, apples, nuts and Christmas cookies with hot choco-late – what a feast.

Next came *Bescherung* – gift giving. We each received one gift, one pair of socks, leggings, mittens, a hat or scarf, a night-gown, or pajamas for the boys. Everything was handmade by either our mother or grandmother. I don't remember the adults ever receiving gifts. I also don't remember any of them ever look-ing sad or upset about it. They actually smiled – which was rare, as I never saw the adults smile much during that time.

This was the only night we could stay up late – way until the morning hours, eating, drinking and telling stories full of adven-tures and laughing. We didn't sing any more songs. It would be late by now and we didn't want to wake our landlord living upstairs. Besides we had sung enough already and the next day – Christmas Day we would be able to sing to our hearts content.

In Germany, they celebrate both the first and second day of Christmas which gives everyone enough time to visit both sides of the family and continue to eat, drink, sing and share stories. Everyone you encountered during that time would wish "*Frohe Weihnachten*" – no exceptions, even your not-so-good friends. That's just how it was.

One of our friends got a new sled and shared it with us so we could go zooming down the hills – either the *Vogelbuck* or the short bunny hill behind the sawmill. This last one was a very tricky ride. Short and steep you had to break really hard at the bottom so as not to hit a tree or break through the frozen brook just beyond. One time I crashed into another sled, injuring my leg. My friends took me on someone else's sled all the way home. This however, did not stop me from taking on the hill again next winter – just like any other kid in the village would have done.

Winter was serene in the country. The village sitting in a ravine all clean and white with snow was surrounded by a collar of forest. Before the snow came and the fields were frozen hard, the village hunters would announce the annual wild boar hunt. This was quite a spectacle. My brothers so looked forward to it. All the young men and older boys would enter the woods making loud noises by shouting and banging sticks together to chase the wild pigs out into the open fields. The hunters would lay in wait for the kill. The next day the villagers would come out to the forester's yard to purchase a segment of the wild pigs. These pork chops were unbelievable. Not a speck of fat. So tender and delicious.

Chapter 3

Home for a Little While

We had received letters from our many relatives throughout Germany about their plans to immigrate to America. Our kin and elders in Wettringen were anxious to join them. Germany was overcrowded and there was a scarcity of good paying jobs. The prospect of ever having anything to truly call our own was bleak at that time. So our aunts, uncles, parents and grandparents were feverishly filling out forms and questionnaires and hoping to hear soon from the authorities of their status in crossing the ocean. Some of our relatives had already been granted permission and our families wanted to join them in this adventure.

I didn't really understand the fascination with all of this. Hadn't we gone through enough changes and upheaval already? Did we really want to pick up everything yet again and move to a faraway country where we didn't even speak the language? A place that was too big, too hot and too wild – at least according to the Wild West movies we saw about America. I realized we had nothing to show for all the labor of my father, but we seemed safe here and were surprisingly well accepted in this small community of Wettringen – which had been our home for ten years. Our prospects would certainly improve here in time, wouldn't they – especially once all of the siblings graduated school and got jobs in the city. But my father was determined. We would just wait and see what would happen. He kept repeating to us – there will never be wars in America – and that was the most important factor to him and for his family.

In the meantime my sister, Perpetua, was accepted in the girls' school in Schillingsfürst. I was somewhat envious at first, but really had no say in the matter and eventually got over it. For my young brothers, life was a piece of cake – school in the morning and then free to roam around to their hearts' content in the wide open spaces, the forests and *Landschaft* surrounding our village.

Meanwhile, I was occupied helping out after school with our first landlord who had an inn/restaurant and a farm. There was always something to do like cleaning the dishes, helping in the garden, peeling potatoes, or apples, feeding the chickens. Frau Moenikheim would give me a bushel of whatever was being harvested at the time. Sometimes I would get a large loaf of bread, especially if it was weekend. Our mother was always thankful for these kind gestures toward us.

During the summer months, I would help my friend Annie with chores in their gardens or fields. For this too, I would get a basket of berries or potatoes or maybe some eggs. Our teacher grew young willow plants near the *TauberSee* – which was really more of a pond than a sea. When they reached a certain height we would harvest the branches which would make fine baskets. During the final months of school we had to decide where we would attend the next phase of education. For me higher learning in the big city was out of the question. Though the schooling was mostly free, the room and board we could not afford.

At the same time there was an apprenticeship opening down the street from us. This consisted of a bakery/grocery store and warehouse. Father said that in times like these, I could always find a good paying job in commerce. I could also take the train one day a week to Rothenburg for business classes – typing, shorthand, bookkeeping, math, advertising, etc. That sounded better – to be able to go to school in this beautiful city. That I could do. I was enamored with that city from my first time there. It was when my sister and I had been confirmed at St. Johannes church.

I liked working with food and dealing directly with customers was also appealing to me. I was accepted as the apprentice and likewise was enrolled at the *Kaufmännisch Berufschule* in Rothenburg. I would also get a stipend of 10DM per month and free meals from the apprenticeship. The U.S. dollar to the Deutsche Mark was at that time 1–4 so that translates to about $2.25 per month – just to give you an idea. To me, at the time however, it seemed like a good deal – coming from a situation where I had never received money before in my life. I was on my way to becoming rich soon – so I thought. In order to work in this establishment, I had to have a health checkup which was mandatory. I passed with a clean bill of health. If only all my tests would be that easy!

Before the end of summer, my father's sister, Tante Monica and Onkel Alois and their families received their confirmation papers for entry into the U.S. Our family had not heard anything yet. Father, disappointed for us, but glad for them, hoped our papers would come shortly. We finally did get the news a few days later. We were turned down. The quota was reached but we could apply again in two years.

Father grew red in the face. He was outraged. Other relatives had made the cut. Why not us? How were we different? In hindsight, grandmother was probably right – they take only the young, strong and the healthy ones. In my family, there were too many dependents, too young to take a job and too many old people with my grandmother in poor health. We were not good prospects to invite into this vast opportunity, that's what I was led to believe. It was certainly not the lack of determination on our parents' part. Our folks had traveled much more difficult roads and had prevailed.

The departure of our kin from the small town was a sad day for our family but most especially for my parents and grandparents. The children, ignorant of the political and bureaucratic wrangling going on, were a source of comfort to my parents and those left behind. The everyday routine was resumed but you could see my father was deeply upset. His dreams were shattered for us.

On top of that, my youngest brother, Al was bitten by a neighbor's dog. Al was about five or six years old at the time and running through farm buildings looking for short cuts. As dogs never resist this temptation, they chased down Al and bit him right in the rear end. What a spectacle – my father and the owner of the dog, *Brillentrump* (there were two farmers in the town named Trump and since this one wore glasses, and the German word for glasses is *Brillen*, ergo – *Brillentrump*), were engaged in a fierce shouting match. There was no such thing as lawsuits in those days – shouting over the fence was the only remedy. Mother tended to little Lois, and of course, he recovered, but he was forever, "reminded" and not so delicately, by his friends of this little escapade.

By this time, summer was coming to an end and I was onto the next chapter of my life. I was already familiar with the place I was to apprentice as we had shopped there before. I also was well acquainted with the owners – naturally in a small town, everyone knows everyone. The owner's youngest son, Rudy also was a classmate of mine and so this made it not so strange to work there. The lady of the house, Frau Vogt, was very kind though she appeared somewhat overworked. Little wonder – she had five sons and no daughters. Her first son had been killed in the war, two were bakers, one was studying at the university and the youngest was to become a baker, but as was customary here, he had to serve his apprenticeship in an out-of-town accredited bakery. Herr Vogt's son, the master baker, ran the store and his brother also worked in the bakery with another classmate of mine, who like me was serving his apprenticeship here. One could not hire or teach apprentices unless you yourself were a master in the craft.

Life soon took on a much faster pace. We started at the crack of dawn to get the goods to the outlying communities. The company's blue VW bus was outfitted with numerous shelves which were filled as soon as the pretzels and *Brötchen* came out of the oven. One of the sons served as the driver and off he went to bring the still warm breads to our customers. Once the bus was out on the road we could take a breather, have a bit of breakfast ourselves and then open for business. During the busy seasons before Christmas and Easter, we would have more helpers assisting with making chocolate Easter bunnies and Santa's. It was a hectic time most certainly.

For almost the entire first year I was not allowed to handle the money, nor anything else for that matter without someone looking over my shoulder. Either the owner, his wife, or his oldest son who was now running the business, would keep their eye on me. They were all very nice to me and often Frau Vogt would give me whatever rolls or baked goods were left at closing. In the summer they even gave me the leftover ice cream which was an even greater treat for my siblings. This bit of extra food was helpful, no, needed by my family.

My first day of trade school was approaching and though I was excited to be able to take the train to Rothenburg, I was a little nervous. To enter that new environment, where I'd never been before, was a bit scary. But how hard could that be? They also spoke German, right?

That day my father walked to work so that I could take the bicycle to the train station. From there it was sheer pleasure, riding on the train through that picturesque landscape to a wondrous city. Rothenburg, I had learned, was a city over a thousand years old, with a multi-colored history, one could write volumes of books without ever boring the reader. I was awed by this old, well preserved, medieval city enclosed by fortified walls and dotted with towers, gates and bridges over the now overgrown moats, remnants of the many wars and territorial feuds that had been fought here.

Inside the walls I saw streets which were narrow, more like our present day alleys. There were cobblestones everywhere. I also visited the very famous market square that entices tourists from all over the world to sightsee and shop and of course see the notorious *Meistertrunk* whose story would be played out every day at noon. As the story goes, the *Bürgermeister* would have to drink a large *Krug* of wine in order for his city to avoid being burned to the ground. Nice benefit of the job!

All the businesses were geared toward hospitality – hotels, restaurants, museums, galleries. However, the bakeries and shoe stores outnumbered all of the other businesses. It must have been the cobblestones – at least to explain the overabundance of shoe stores. As for the bakeries, well, breakfast at that time always included fresh rolls – sometimes cereal and soft boiled eggs but always fresh rolls.

The business trade school was located straight across town from the train station very near the old *Burggarten* – fortress garden. The walk back and forth to school never bothered me. It was always such a colorful sight. Quaint and bustling with activity, it was sincerely a pleasure to be part of it all. It was also a very romantic city. I was reminded of so many books I had read – fairy tales.

I think I spent the happiest days of my youth here. My classmates were much more tolerant of my foreign status, but then maybe I really wasn't all that foreign. Right from the start I befriended a young girl in class named Ehmann's Traudl. She became my closest friend during my time there and still remains so. I've never forgotten our repeated lunch exchanges in the middle of this pretty school courtyard. In the middle ages it was a convent churchyard, gated with wrought iron gates and spilling out to a most beautiful view of the valley below. It was customary that the bakeries would alternate weekly delivering goods to our school. Traudl's brother was a baker apprentice. At lunchtime, he would come with a large basket on his back and place it on the lowest corner of the wall and sell the fresh baked rolls and pretzels to us.

Traudl and I mostly brought our own sandwiches from home. We would then exchange them – her *Brötchen* with butter and sausage for my rye bread with *Schmaltz* and sometime some *Wurst*. It's funny what sticks out in your mind over the years. After classes, I would have some time until the next train home. It was then Traudl gave me tours of the famous and the not-so-famous places in town. We would explore so many nooks in the town most tourists had not time to see. I was often overwhelmed by all that she showed me; she was the most knowledgeable and interesting tour guide.

Christmas time in Rothenburg was awesome. The market square was transformed into a winter wonderland. All the merchants from the more distant locations would bring their wares to the center of town and display their specialties in one of many wooden stalls that filled the market place. The different foods and smells created a fantastic cloud that wafted through the entire city. Then came the snow and the city was transformed into a twentieth century fairyland. Beautiful music spilled out from every church and concert hall. On the street corners, musicians would play the familiar Christmas melodies. Strolling children in period costumes sang carols following a lone youngster carrying a stick or pole dangling a star through the narrow alleys. Almost every window displayed a *Tannenbaum* or candles glowing, inviting you in. It was so heartwarming. I didn't want it to end.

From my standpoint, life was good here. It did not really matter that we didn't have our own home or for that matter, my own room, or private bathroom. We had an outhouse. It was the closeness of my family that mattered most. I wasn't bitter about my family's situation but I cannot speak for my siblings – I don't know how they felt during this time, but they were fairly young at that time. My parents, of course, felt totally different for reasons I didn't then understand, but do now. Like the old saying goes: ignorance is bliss.

One day in the spring of 1953 I was called home by one of my brothers. My grandmother had died. Her heart had finally given out. As I walked in everyone was gathered upstairs around her bed, praying and crying. She was most certainly in a better place, for she had been sick for as long as I could remember yet kept trying to keep our morale up during our most trying times. As I saw her, my thoughts went back a few weeks while she was still alive. She became more helpless but could not thank my mother often enough for caring for her so diligently.

I remember vividly one evening, after mother had bathed her in our kitchen, bent over an old tin bathtub with my large grandfather holding a sheet around them for privacy. He had carried her upstairs as she was partially paralyzed but before he passed through the door my mother held open, I heard him say to my mother," and to think, so long ago, we didn't want you as our daughter-in-law." I guess he had wanted a richer girl for his son. You see, my mother came from a very large family with eight brothers and she being the only daughter, her portion amounted to little. To me, mother was the perfect woman any man would want and that day, I think my grandfather finally realized it.

The funeral brought many of my grandmother's relatives from across the country to us. These cousins, brothers, aunts and uncles, along with the many villagers, accompanied her to the cemetery next to the church where she would finally rest.

After her passing everything seemed so strange. I couldn't wait for my sister to return from the convent so that I would have someone to talk to about all that had happened. We always had so much to talk about at bed time. More than once Father would call out to us to hush. We would continue to whisper under the blanket. This would be interrupted every now and then with an "ouch" as an errant piece of straw would stick one of us. We would giggle and then continue. We didn't have mattresses. Our beds were made of straw and in the morning we would make our beds by reaching into the large burlap sacks and loosening the straw. After the harvest, we would get new straw and with a flannel sheet over it, provided a very comfortable bed.

We never took a vacation. First of all we were always busy. No one else took off. It would be a very outlandish thing to do that would start people talking. We really didn't know what we were missing.

Periodically we would get packages from Tante Monika Bernhard, who had already immigrated to America, which were always much appreciated – mostly clothing and sometimes yards of beautiful material for dresses for my sister and me. I remember once in particular, both of us got look-a-like white and lilac plaid dresses with a soft black bow at the collar. These packages, however, opened new wounds for my father. He did not like charity. Even though we could use this help, he was still bitter in feeling we were somehow not good enough for America. Our other relatives had been accepted and we had not. So, once again, he applied for entry, hoping for the best. The children were never consulted in this matter. Whenever my parents had conversations in Rumanian, I suspected the topic was none of our business. These conversations happened more regularly after the packages arrived.

It was not then a big surprise to me when we again began the process of filling out applications for immigration to America again. Father was hopeful. This would be it. My sister and I were nearly done with our schooling and able to work. We were no longer so many dependents which had been a big stumbling block in our previous quest. Grandmother was no longer with us. It's almost prophetic what she had so often said. That she had held us back – had been a burden to us. Father waited in anticipation.

My mother was a very quiet person. She was here for us only it seemed. She hardly ever uttered her own preferences or wishes. I don't know how she felt about moving to America or how my siblings felt about it. We never spoke about it. However, my grandfather and I were none too pleased about the prospect of moving. He often said, "One does not transplant an old tree."

Another summer came and went when we finally received a letter from immigration bureau saying we were now being considered as possible émigrés. Father was thrilled. Grandfather and I were not. The rest of the family had no reaction – was it shock? Or did they really not understand what was going on because they were so young. It would not have mattered how we felt in any event, for as children we really had no input in these adult matters. We could not speak unless spoken to.

We also never saw much affection played out between parents and children or even couples as we do now. It was improper. By that, I don't mean to say we were not loved by our parents – on the contrary, we were loved and appreciated, but this love was not shown publicly. For that matter, one would not speak to others about "crushes." It would always be a big surprise for the village when so-and-so was getting married to so-and-so.

As I got older, I too developed a crush, just as my friends had. I was a late bloomer and kept this secret to myself. It was a hopeless case, anyway. That much I had determined from overhearing other's conversations. There were no reciprocal feelings from the boy I had a crush on. He was a native boy, and I was a foreigner, a refugee. On top of that, we were not of the same faith. This was paramount. It was best not to spend too much time and energy on that prospect. You go about your life as before and sooner or later you get over it. We would soon be going to America with all of those complications. This would be one less thing to worry about.

My graduation was nearing and as much as I was looking forward to it, I also wished it would somehow be postponed as I so enjoyed school. Graduation itself came and went without pomp and circumstance, no party, no grand celebrations, instead we left school and sometime thereafter, our diploma would be sent to us in the mail. I had hoped to get a job after graduation in one of the many delicatessens in Rothenburg but that was a faraway dream. On that last day of school, Traudl and I walked the narrow cobblestone streets searching for possible places looking for that delicatessen or food store where I might be able to get that job. We walked so long that day I missed the last train home.

Traudl told me I could spend the night at her house and in the morning take the first train home. Since we didn't have a phone at our home, I called the local grocery store to have them let my parents know. We were about to retire, when Traudl's mother appeared and informed us that someone from Wettringen was outside to give me a ride home on his motorcycle. Who would do that? There weren't that many motorcycles in our tiny town. I was astounded to see that same young man, the one I had had that crush on – sitting patiently on his bike with the motor running. I was a bit worried however, getting on this motorcycle given my past experience with bicycles let alone this motorcycle.

I felt scared and most probably showed it. Traudl assured me it was probably safe and the rider smiled at this. He was not one of those wilder riders, well known in our village and I got on the motorcycle and held on tight per his instructions. I felt myself blushing. Zooming over the cobblestones, leaning the wrong way into the turns, I finally got the hang of it and calmed down. Once out of town everything got pitch black, and then we zoomed through the forests and up and down hills. When a car came toward us I felt surely we would be hit as the roads were so very narrow. At least it did not rain. And before I knew it we were home.

At the gate I thanked the driver kindly and he put his arms around me and kissed me. Shook up, I ran inside and slammed the front door. This was a ritual. I always slammed the door. Riding my bicycle home from the train at night those many nights, I was petrified. I would just ride the bike as fast as I could to my house, drop it in the front and burst into the house slamming the door behind me. My father would then go outside and put the bicycle away. But this time, I wasn't panting out of fright, but of total surprise. I couldn't believe he liked me back nor did I think he was being fresh. I kept this to myself. This experience I could only share with my sister who was due to come home for the summer very soon. She was my only confidante.

It had been a privilege to attend school in Rothenburg and live in Wettringen. It wasn't always easy, but most good things don't come easy, or do they? Just as things started looking brighter, we were informed we would have to report to Munich in one month. We needed to be checked out to make certain we were all healthy enough to make the journey and that all our papers were in order.

It seemed odd that we were instructed to go south to Munich when all of our other relatives had gone north to Bremerhaven on the North Sea for their point of departure. This was however, the elder's concern, not ours. Just as we were preparing for the big move, my brother Adi, who was preparing to graduate the eighth grade, received a letter from a prominent technical school in Nürnberg letting him know that he had been accepted. He was surprised since the exam was difficult and so many had applied. But now, what good was this to him when we were all set to leave for a faraway country, certain never to return? Had he been older, I'm certain Adi would have remained to continue his studies, but this was not meant to be. My whole world was in upheaval. Packing and selling the few pieces of furniture we had, we prepared for the big move.

At the upstairs hall at Moenikheim's, the villagers threw us a farewell party – this same hall had been our first shelter when we arrived in Wettringen in August, 1945. The party was fun but also very sad. The old shoemaker said, the next day in the store as I waited on him. "You know, Milleri," (they never addressed you by your first name here once you were past childhood – since our last name was Mueller, the females in the family would be called *Muellerin*, or *Milleri*, in the local dialect.) "You know, Milleri, you didn't have to go to America. You could have gotten a husband here also."

That did it. This assured me that indeed the villagers had accepted us as their equals, even though it had taken ten years.

They no longer saw us as strangers or refugees. This was wonderful to me. That night after I told my parents about this, they were surprised and pleased. This however, did not change anything, our plans were in motion and our departure date was set for July 14, 1955. That night I cried. It was strange, for I had not cried since I was maybe ten years old when I had had nightmares and would wind up in my parents' bed.

On one of my last trips to Rothenburg before we would have to appear in Munich for our journey to the U.S., Traudl and I took a last stroll, through Rothenburg. We had chocolate at the *Plönlein* and ice cream at the *Eis Diele* behind the *Kapellenplatz*. I had a hard time holding my feelings in. At the train station I wanted to weep as we said *Auf Wiedersehen*. We both tried to help each other by saying this separation would not be forever. The train ride home was so bleak. It seemed there would be no tomorrow, at least as I knew it. Even the rainiest of days in Wettringen seemed cheerful now. In Gailnau our train stopped. I picked up my bicycle, it was dark now and I headed home. Although my bicycle light was lit, there was gravel and loose stones and holes the entire way. The only border saving you from coming off the road was formed by tall poplar trees lining the road. You could see these dark and foreboding shadows. As I mentioned before, I was always afraid of the dark and raced home as fast as I could. This night however, I was surprised on the road by an oncoming pedestrian. I could hear the footsteps on the gravel and told myself not to panic. There was no crime in this corner of the world. I knew everyone here.

As this person came closer I heard my name called out. It was my secret crush. He wanted to walk me home to say a final goodbye. I was thrilled but sad and cried the rest of the way home. He pushed my bike with one hand and put his arm around me the whole time home. It seemed so tragic and I've never forgotten this. After that last embrace and a kiss, I would never see him again.

On the day of our departure, my boss took us to the train in his blue Volkswagen. As we drove through the village along the familiar countryside, it was eerily still. You could only hear an occasional and repressed sob. This was supposed to be a happy time for us yet no one was laughing or even smiling. This was just another road on our family's long journey.

Chapter 4

A Whole New World

The long train ride to Munich passed in stillness. Everyone seemed wrapped in their thoughts and feelings. Even the boys were somewhat subdued – unnatural for them. Adi was fourteen, Tony was thirteen and Al was ten. They were usually a loud and boisterous bunch especially on an adventure such as this. I took inventory staring out the window. I had hours and hours to contemplate my future. What were these Americans like? Will they like us? Will we like them? We don't speak English, how would this work out? Then again, if our relatives in Chicago could overcome this, why shouldn't we be able to? This will be a transition for us for sure. From what we had learned in geography, it would be much hotter than we were accustomed to. In the end I thought, we would do just fine, particularly if the people we met would be similar to the GI's we encountered right after the war when I was only a child, seven at most, but their kindness and compassion left a lasting impression on me. Through the most turbulent times, their outreach to us was touching and deeply appreciated.

In Munich we were taken to a large complex looking like military barracks. Here we were to report for paper inspections and physical checkups. After everything was approved, one of the female officers asked our mother through an interpreter, if she would be willing to help transport a baby. The baby's name was Judy. The officer said, having raised five children my mom would be an ideal person to take this child in transit to the States. The baby would be picked up upon arrival in New York. Mother, of course, said yes. That raised a question: were we going to fly to the USA? This would be different for certain. The boys were getting so excited. We had assumed all along we would be going by boat just as our other relatives had.

The next day it rained and was cold. Wearing our raincoats, we were taken early in the morning to the Munich airport. The plane was a troop transporter. The seats were close together and it was very barren inside. The plane however was full. There were even some soldiers on it. It was both scary and exciting. This was our very first flight. No one had ever been this close to an airplane or an airport for that matter. It was a propeller type aircraft, in stark contrast to the luxury planes we use nowadays. It felt strange flying and my stomach was a bit queasy. However, the baby kept us distracted from our more immediate surroundings. She cried most of the time. Mother, Perpetua and I took turns walking and cuddling her. She was sweet, but what baby is not? Suddenly the flight got a bit bumpy and the girls thought the worse. What did we know about planes or flying or bumps? Someone said we were crossing the English Channel and that the bumps were normal. I'm not sure the baby or I was convinced!

Our first stop was in England, though I don't remember what airport or town. We needed to refuel before heading over the Atlantic. To think, we would be crossing the mighty body of water we had studied in geography at school – this was awesome. Soon we were given small boxes of sandwiches and juice. Grandfather was the first to question the food. He said, "Are you sure this is bread, it looks like it's not fully baked yet and it's sticking to the roof of my mouth?"

The boys ate the crust only because the middle was too soft. The bread on the farms was dark and hard, and this soft white bread was nothing like we knew of bread. We worried a little of things to come based on this first tasting of American cuisine.

Next we landed in Reykjavik, Iceland. It was really cold with rain, rain and more rain. We disembarked and were sent to a place where we could get some food and stretch our legs a bit. You couldn't see much of the town and only when we took off again could we glimpse a bit of it, then white, then ocean again. Grandfather kept holding his ears. They gave us some gum to try to alleviate the pain but he didn't know gum. We had a lot of fun watching him maneuver the gum around his mouth until he got the hang of it.

We next landed in Newfoundland. We thought we had arrived but we were only there to refuel. They told us our next stop would be LaGuardia Airport in New York. From there we were to be driven to another airport named Idlewild (which is now Kennedy Airport). At this point we were all becoming restless and nervous.

All these people coming and going, was my first impression on landing in New York... and you couldn't understand a word passing between them. An official led us to a spot where we delivered baby Judy to the authorities and said our goodbyes. Funny how close you can get to someone in such a short time. Then again, how difficult is it to love a little baby? In hindsight, I'm sure everything was proper and legal, at least everything appeared so.

In the bus it was so very, very hot. Although all the windows were open, there was no breeze at all. We were miserable. We had expected heat but not this much. It didn't even compare to our hottest summers working in the fields back home. We arrived at the next airport and here we would await our flight to Chicago. Good thing there were some kind people around showing us where to wait. It took a while waiting on this connecting flight and my brothers became restless. My father warned them not to wander off to far – not to get lost among all these travelers. Not long after Adi and Anthony took off, exploring, I suppose. They seemed to be gone for a while and upon their return, my father gave them a stern reprimand. They told us of a most unusual encounter.

They came upon a large standup box and a person put a coin in it and something fell down. I can just imagine them standing there with their mouths open. As they marveled at this apparatus, another man came closer – a young black man. He did the same thing, but as that something came down, he collected it, opened it, and gave it to the boys. He smiled at them, and gestured as if drinking. It was their first Coke. Was it so obvious we were foreigners? Wow, what a welcome.

Finally, we were led to the United Airlines gate and ushered in. This was completely different from our first flight. They put us in a cabin all to ourselves. The seats were padded like living room furniture and the food was excellent. Although our stomachs were still queasy, we appreciated this much more comfortable airplane. At first we thought all the non-military planes were outfitted like this, only later did we learn we had traveled in a first class cabin. I still wonder why we had received the royal treatment. After all we had not done anything extraordinary to deserve this. Were all immigrants welcomed like this?

Of course we couldn't ask them this as we knew nothing of the English language. We conversed in hand movements and nods or shakes of the head. It's amazing what one can communicate with only smiles and goodwill. We flew over the eastern part of the country when down below we began to see the Great Lakes that let us know we were almost there. It's a good thing to pay attention in geography class. You never know when it will come in handy and for us it most certainly did then.

Soaring over Lake Michigan and seeing the city of Chicago down below was exciting. Descending down into Midway Airport, we could see all these colorful dots, like marbles surrounding the airport. As we came lower, we could see they were cars. How could there be so many cars in one place? I could not believe it. Does everyone, everyone drive a car? Is there any room for people who walk?

We landed; and as we were ushered through the airport, we spied some of our relatives who had come to meet us with tears running down their cheeks. I don't remember if suitcases were opened and checked, I just remember rushing out to the exits with all our family. Here, everyone old and young was kissing and embracing us, though most of them I didn't recognize. I had only known these folks from photos and stories. Our parents knew them. But their children, who were now teenagers, we really didn't know. Many of them had been born in transit, from Rumania, Czechoslovakia; Austria, Yugoslavia and Germany. We never got to know each other in Europe. We had all been scattered throughout Germany after the war.

I only knew Tante Monika and her family, and Onkel Alois and his family as they had lived for a while in our village in Wettringen and had immigrated to the U.S. before us. After all this hugging and crying we were divided into several cars and driven to Onkel Otto's house. We were to reside on the third floor of a large greystone flat. Onkel Otto was my mother's older brother.

It was even hotter in Chicago. It must have been 100 degrees on that day, July 15, 1955. We could not unpack even a little, as my uncle's wife Tante Monika had cooked all day preparing for our arrival. So much food, so much rich food, we were not accustomed to. Relatives packed the apartment wall-to-wall, with everyone talking at the top of their lungs. The feast went on and on and after everyone left I could not distinguish which face belonged to which cousin, or which cousin belonged to which Tante or Onkel.

Our flat was mostly furnished. Our relatives had pooled together beds, chairs, a table, and bedding and had put food in our refrigerator. Though we never had one of those back home, but in this heat, I could see a refrigerator was a necessity. It was late and finally everyone was gone. Not that we didn't appreciate all this celebration and hospitality but we needed to slow down, to rest. Our stomachs were still sensitive, all that rich food, and this unbearable heat – we were all a bit overdone. As much as we needed a good night's sleep this was not to happen during this exceptionally stifling heat wave.

Our grandfather was whisked away by our father's sister, Tante Monika to live with them. This was a provision under which he was able to come with us to America so that he would not count as a financial burden to our large family. Our greystone apartment was on Belmont between Leavitt and Hoyne and grandfather would live near Damen and Belle Plaine. This wasn't too bad. Once he had the directions figured out, he would walk over to our home every day.

I remember the weeks after our arrival as one very long vacation. Every day we were invited to some cousin's, Tante's or Onkel's for dinner. I don't think my mom cooked for the first month we had arrived. During the days some of our cousins or second cousins spread across the Lakeview neighborhood, would drive us around after work to the nearest schools for the boys and to possible job sites for the rest of us.

The school part was relatively easy for the boys. Jahn's Elementary School was right behind us. Adi and Tony later went to Lane Tech and Al later went to St. Benedicts as we moved around as well. My sister and I went to night school at Lakeview High School at Irving Park and Ashland. We learned English and civics to prepare to take an exam to become U.S. citizens. We could all walk to the school and our teacher there was superb. His name was Mr. Swanson and our classes consisted of mostly German and Greek immigrants. Some of the students were quite old. Mr. Swanson loved to sing and after reciting the Pledge of Allegiance we would sing patriotic songs, first the national anthem, then "My Country, 'Tis of Thee", "America the Beautiful" and I thought that was such a smart way to teach the language. Once you know the melody, the words come easier, like rhymes and poems.

On Sunday, our cousins downstairs took us to their church, St. Alphonsus. It was not far from the apartment and from a distance it looked very much like a church from home. The imposing veranda was a perfect gathering spot before and after mass. Also, just like home. Entering into the church was overwhelming. It was beautiful. I could not have pictured such a beautiful gothic church in America. All we knew about America was what we saw in the Wild West, John Wayne movies and books. Wide open prairies and large masses of cattle, that's how I had envisioned the States.

The mass was conducted entirely in German! This amazed me. The hymns and sermon, and the entire mass were in German. My parents had tears streaming down their faces. We had not expected this. It made me respect the tolerance of these Americans. After mass, people would stand around in little groups and exchange news and information with the newcomers.

The veranda, just above the street, was perfect for these social exchanges.

Our "old world" tradition of having our Sunday dinner at noon continued here. After the meal our cousins would take us to Montrose Beach. That would become our favorite Sunday after-noon destination – that is, if our jobs would allow it – those that had jobs. The rest of us were still desperately searching.

At that time, our Onkel Florian (my mother's youngest brother), worked for Schillmoeller and Krofl, a construction firm where he was also able to find work for some of our newly arrived relatives. My father was lucky enough to be one of them. At the time they were building a new church in the "boonies" they said. In those days, a suburb called Skokie seemed so far out in the middle of nowhere. Our mother too, soon found work in a casting factory where some of our cousins worked. Her nephew, Frank, lived just downstairs and could drive. Because he was one of our only relatives to own a car, he would bring a carload to and from work every day. In those days you could pile six and even seven passengers in a car, seatbelts were not an issue.

My sister, who was about sixteen at the time, found a job across the street at a grocery store. I was still looking for some-thing in my field. My cousin Pete would take me to several of the many German stores up and down Lincoln Ave. All of them turned me down as I couldn't speak any English. I was getting disillusioned when my cousin Agie asked me to go with her to the beauty shop where she worked. Maybe they would have a job for me. They did – as a manicurist, at a lovely little shop in Rogers Park near Loyola University.

It wasn't what I was trained for, but it was a job and I was glad to have it. The people here were just wonderful and patient – the customers were tolerant and kind. The owner, Maxine Robinson was a most out-going and gracious woman. She could not have been more kind and supportive. Strange as it is to admit, I was a bit surprised by this as we had heard that the blacks and whites in America did not always get along. But from the American soldiers that first shared their fruits and chocolates with us, to that winking man in New York who gave my brothers their first Coke, to my first boss – these people could not have been nicer to us. I was surprised, but then again, not so surprised. Maybe the newspapers had it all wrong – maybe it was wrong what we heard.

It was difficult working all day and going to school at night but so many of our people were in the same situation. On my days off, I would do the laundry in the basement. On one such day I was working with the wringer washer (which was new to us) and got my hand stuck in the wringer while straightening a pair of jeans. Luckily, the wringer popped open just before it got to my wrist. It didn't hurt, but it did get rid of a knot that kept popping up on my hand – saved us a trip to the hospital in more ways than one.

The boys could walk to school and were soon speaking English. It bothered me that they could speak better than me. In time, I was certain, I would be just as good. Or so I thought.

After about two years of frugal saving by all of my family's wage earners, we were able to pool enough money to put a down payment on our first home – my father's American dream, a two-flat brick house on Cullom, between Lincoln and Damen. At the same time three of our uncles bought similar properties on the same block. It was just like back home in Rumania before the war. Even though our English was getting better every day – it was so much more comfortable having our relatives just down the street. It was easier for our grandfather too – living on Belle Plaine – this was closer and we would see him more often.

One evening, my cousin Felizitas, who was also named after my maternal grandmother, invited me to accompany her to choir practice at St. Alphonsus church. Since I always sang, as early as kindergarten, I was excited to come along. I liked it right from the start. There were so many young people so full of energy and laughter. Most of them were all German immigrants, like me. They had come to Chicago from the Balkans, the then Yugoslavia, Rumania, Hungary, Austria and some, of course, Germany.

Our director was from Tirol, a part of Austria. Alfred Schoepko had come to Chicago via California and had just accepted the position of director of the German choir of St. Alphonsus church. While continuing his studies at Northwestern University, he was willing to teach these exuberant students beautiful sacred music. All these untamed music lovers were hard to resist – so I too joined this noisy bunch of singers.

Most of the girls from the choir had attended high school at St. Alphonsus and seemed very much at home here. It did not take long before I felt most comfortable among them. Some of the young men came from the local German social clubs, like the Donauschwaben, and the Aid Society of German Descendents, while another group of them came from the Kolping Haus on Wellington and Halsted. Adolf Kolping was the founder of this organization that provided a home away from home for young men where they could live until they were on their feet or got married. Mr. and Mrs. Hild served as surrogate parents to these young boarders.

These young men quickly formed a tight friendship. We would often go to the Kolping Haus after choir practice and play table tennis. Meals were prepared by Frau Hild who would often have refreshments ready for us after choir. One of the young men, Alfred Mayer took on the role as chef, which stuck with him throughout his stay. Here we had some really great times.

We learned so many beautiful songs for the German mass on Sundays. And it was not only sacred music that we learned but also classical pieces and German *Lieder*. Soon we were invited to participate in concerts at other German festivals. On one such concert we sang the Schubert Dances among the many *Lieder*. Of all the years growing up in Germany, I had never heard of them. I had to come to America to be introduced to it! We also learned many Christmas hymns and lullabies. They were wonderful. I was amazed and loved being part of these concerts.

Within only two years of my joining the choir, we performed probably our most ambitious work, a concert with members of the Chicago Symphony Orchestra and member soloists. At the then St. Alphonsus Athenaeum, we performed Mozart's Coronation Mass under the direction of Alfred Schoepko, our director. The performance also included Mozart's *Ave Verum* and *Eine Kleine Nachtmusik*. I didn't think we could pull it off. One of the most distinguished players that played with us was Ray Still, the famous oboist – it was really awesome. Thanks to Herr Schoepko's direction and confidence in us, it was one of the most memorable and moving concerts we were able to perform.

Those were great times. No one had much "stuff" in those days. Many didn't even have a car. Those that had would pile in as many as they could and then drive us all home after practices and performances. On the weekends, there were always celebrations at Weberhalle or at some club or another and we would gather and just dance the night away. The young men would stand on one side of the wall and the girls on the opposite side. As soon as the music started, the boys would charge across the hall to grab the prettiest girl. Mostly there were enough so that every girl could get a partner. Sometimes though, there were a few "extra" girls and you didn't want to be one of those.

It seems silly now, but back then these dances were serious competition. What was interesting, I don't ever remember anyone ever talking about working out, but then, who needed, it with all the dancing we did on Saturday and Sunday nights. The slowest dance was probably the tango or the English waltz. All the others were fast and even dizzying at times – waltzes, swing, the fox trot, and polkas – what fun. The strange thing was that there were no "steady" couples at that time. Everyone was single and happy about it. At the end of the evening, there was always a huge table full of homemade food prepared by mothers doubling as chaperones. The young ladies would help serve. There were not just sandwiches, but schnitzel, pork roasts, bratwurst, potato salad and spätzle, homemade cakes and tortes. It was as good as any wedding banquet.

Some of the young men had returned from serving in the armed forces and our choir had grown to 50 members strong. It was just about then that the "pairing up" started. The tenors would court the sopranos; the basses would court the altos. The weddings started shortly thereafter. Some years we celebrated three weddings which always included a performance by the choir. Naturally, you could not wear the same dress to these weddings, especially where there was three or four in one year. My own wedding was the best, of course. Here again, the talented mothers would come to the rescue and design and sew beautiful one-of-a-kind fancy dresses for the occasion. How lucky for us!

My own wedding luncheon was celebrated at our two-flat in October of 1957. The lucky groom – was Richard. Also a member of the choir, he had served in Korea, had come to Chicago and moved into the Kolping Haus with all those handsome young men who had joined the choir. Watching them strutting down Wellington, we would gaze at these sharp, well-dressed men making their way to the church. They laughed all the time. Suits, long coats and of course, a Stetson hat, they were as handsome as any movie star of the time.

Richard had a beautiful tenor voice. He was charming but could also be brash at times. It didn't take long before we were an item. We were maybe the fifth or sixth "couple" produced from this choir. The wedding was beautiful. The choir sang at our church and our reception was held in the evening at the Kolping Haus. Richard's parents flew in from Germany. His cousin, Margret from Canada came with her mother Aloisia and was one of the bridesmaids. The rest of the bridesmaids included my sister (the maid of honor) a good friend of mine, Kaethe Milliker and my cousin, Martha Bachmeier. On the groom's side, Richard's brother Joe served as best man, while his friend Clemens Wohn, and two of my cousins, Jake Ruscheinsky and Alois Soehn made up the rest of the party. Before my bridesmaids and I left for church, my father recited a "mini-rosary," to bless the wedding. This was in accordance with an old world custom. I didn't realize then how much we needed that blessing.

The wedding ceremony itself started out a bit rocky. When I arrived I saw my father pacing back and forth in the back of the church. Nothing was happening. The music was not playing, the groom and the rest of the party was still not lined up at the front of the church. He was worried.

Our choir director, Alfred Schoepko was assigned the duty to pick up Richard from the Kolping Haus. As it turns out, they had been involved in a minor fender bender on the way to church. But none of us knew that at the time. As the minutes clicked by, we all worried with father. Then, before you know it, the boys appeared. The choir sang, the men took their place and the rest of the mass went on without a hitch.

The next order of wedding business was the luncheon at our house. All of the furniture was removed from our living and dining room. Many tables were fitted into a "T" formation stretching through the two rooms. This was not a catered affair; rather the luncheon came with the help of many cousins and sisters-in-law of my mother. They had come the day before and in that single kitchen each had prepared their specialty. They cooked and baked, broiled and braised all day and all night. I remember most especially the soup. I don't know why, maybe because of my nerves. The soup was delicious. About 30 or so people came to the luncheon including Father Thomas, who had performed the ceremony. The main reception was then held at the Kolping Haus with dinner and dancing into way late into the morning. It was loud and the dance floor was always full. We had somewhere between 200–250 guests. Most were German immigrants with a smattering of Americans we knew through work.

We probably had one of the more unique honeymoons. The day after the wedding we drove to Florida in a brand new '57 Ford which my husband had purchased just before the wedding. The drive south was for the most part uneventful, other than getting lost somewhere near Chattanooga. We arrived in Daytona Beach and after that first night as husband and wife, we decided to walk down the beach. As we made our way along the beach we could hear voices calling to us along the boardwalk just above us. We looked up and leaning over the railing was Richard's brother with his parents and their Tante Aloisia, grinning from ear to ear. I couldn't believe my eyes! What were they doing here?

I quickly wrapped a towel around my bathing suit. Richard waved at them quite enthusiastically. My father-in-law was beaming. They had rented a little house just behind where they were standing. We spent most of our honeymoon in that house. Tante Aloisia and Sudendorf's mum (that was what my mother-in-law was called back home) made all of our meals. We never once went out for a meal during this honeymoon. One night, I remember, in particular. Tante Aloisia was making white asparagus and needed nutmeg – and nobody knew how to say "nutmeg" in English.

My father-in-law insisted we walk to the store and demand "*Muskatnuss.*" So off we went to the store and asked a young lady for "*Muskatnuss*" using various pronunciations – some stressing the first syllable, some the second and on and on. The lady just shook her head. After smelling various spices we finally found it – nutmeg. This was a source of riotous laughter for years to come during our trips to Germany.

To this day, I don't know if Richard knew about this "surprise" honeymoon visit or not, but we all enjoyed it tremendously.

Chapter 5

New Home, New Family

Our first residence as husband and wife was a small three room apartment in Rogers Park that was near my work. At the time, Richard was working for Stepan Chemical and needed the car to get to work. I could walk to the salon from this apartment and so that was all we needed at that point. Our first child, a girl, Patti was born while we lived here and boy, would she be spoiled!

Every Sunday after mass we would eat dinner at my mom's house. Once the children came, mom would go to the earlier mass so that we could leave the children with her while we attended mass. But as the children became "church trained" we would take them along. This same evolution occurred with all of the choir families and soon many "church trained" children could be seen – and not heard – occupying rows and rows of St. Alphonsus church up in the choir loft. It wasn't long before the children would be singing most of the songs we sang during the masses on our journey home or to Oma's (short for 'old mama's') house. The children called St. Alphonsus – the "eating church." The parish had set up a small coffee shop in a building next to the church where you could get coffee, donuts and a brief visit before heading back home. Naturally, this was a big hit with the kids!

Some church goers came from the far outlying suburbs to attend this German mass. It was a comfort to catch up and exchange news in their native language. Especially for the older people and those of us that spoke very little English – this was a welcome retreat. We really didn't telephone each other much in those days and so this weekly exchange of information provided a much needed network for us. Everyone was appreciative and grateful to the archdiocese for providing this German speaking mass – giving us a connection with our homeland.

My brothers, in the meantime, had enlisted in the armed forces. Al, who joined the army, served two tours in Vietnam. Anthony chose the Navy and was stationed in the Mediterranean Sea. Mother, of course, was not happy with any of this. She had seen most of her brothers sent off to war and one of her brothers, Alex, never returned. Now her own sons were being sent off to war with the uncertainty of their return. At that time, Richard and I and the girls – our family now included two more little girls, first Linda and then Maria – were living in an apartment building my father had purchased on Byron Street in Chicago. We lived in a third floor apartment but spent many hours with my parents who lived below and we saw "Oma" as she cried and cried each time one of her boys left for the war and then even more so, when they returned.

Many of my cousins were serving as well, and all of them returned one by one. Each return marked a cause for celebration. These turned into loud, crowded affairs as each family was fairly large to begin with. This extended family needed a place to accommodate these and other celebrations. They needed a clubhouse. They also needed an outlet for all the extra energy that comes in those turbulent growing up years. They started a soccer team, the Chicago Kickers. Success. The youngsters worked as hard at soccer as their parents worked at providing a safe home and community for their families. It didn't take long for our soccer team to rise to the top, first in their club league and then onto U.S. amateur champs with a trip to Washington D.C. – Bravo, SC Chicago Kickers! During this particular time, the Kickers had been State Champions of Illinois nine times from 1959–1982; League Champions, Indoor League Champions and U.S. Amateur Champions four times from 1966 to 1975.

Both my brothers also made it home safely after serving and our family was once again restored and relieved, my mother most especially. Al actually went to university on the GI Bill at the University of Illinois in Chicago. He was the first in our family to obtain a college degree. He studied engineering and over time was able to start his own business. The boys were all growing up and with that went our babysitters. The children had always looked forward to their uncles' evenings with them. They still talk about the times their uncles would come by with their then-girlfriends. You know how that goes, "when the cat's away…"

Also, during this time, I was preparing to become a U.S. citizen. One of my good friends, Leni from the German choir agreed to be my sponsor. I was quite confident I would pass the test as I constantly read and reread about the three branches of government, U.S. history, which I especially enjoyed, and the U.S. constitution. I also didn't worry as my friends reassured me there was nothing to worry about. So I didn't.

On the day I was to take the test, Leni and I went down to the immigration building, to the room we had been directed toward and I waited for my name to be called out. When they did call out some strange name, I knew it was mine for most Americans could not seem to pronounce my name correctly. I got up and after repeating my name to the clerk, was ushered to a desk and told to sit down. The clerk began paging through some type of folder and looked up every now and then. He finally looked at me directly and asked; "Do you know what a prostitute is?" I couldn't believe what I was hearing. All the topics I had studied for so diligently and this was the stupid question I was being asked. I felt my face getting hot and I just glared at him. He stared back at me and said, "Well?"

I guess he was just not going to drop the subject so I said, "A woman who sleeps with a man for money." He smirked somewhat and scribbled something on the forms. That was all. I was finished. I was furious. I asked myself, "Why had I ever come to this country to be humiliated like that?" After a few days, I was sworn in. A large group of immigrants was sworn in by Judge Freeman at the old McCormick Place. A year or so after, my parents were preparing for their citizenship. Although, I never told them about my own experience – I would have died before I told my parents – I just hoped they wouldn't get the same clerk.

Most of our friends had bought two-flats when they began having families and so did we. On one floor the families would live and the other would be rented out as income. This was a very simple and frugal way to make some money. Ours was on Winthrop Avenue in Rogers Park.

Our family grew on Winthrop, our first son, Richard Jr. joined us in 1966 and this made Richard Sr. very happy. Finally, a boy! We also experienced our first big snow storm. The blizzard of 1967 locked us into our home for days. The kids burrowed snow tunnels from our front sidewalk to the back and spent their days romping through the snow. For them it was great fun. No school. Endless hours of playtime with their neighborhood friends. Not so much for their parents. Grocery stores emptied out. You couldn't find any milk after a day or two. You really felt marooned. Lucky for us a milk truck got stuck right in front of our house and we all ran out and bought milk directly from the truck. This was also a time Richard spent a good part of every week commuting to Ohio for business. He had since gotten a job with Siemen's medical and part of his territory included Ohio. Again, as luck would have it, he was home during that week and got that tunnel started for the kids.

It was while we were living on Winthrop, I also learned to drive. As I mentioned earlier, Richard was traveling a lot with Siemen's between Chicago and Ohio but we managed to squeeze in a couple of driving lessons. This didn't turn out so well. After just a couple of lessons, Richard gave up when I constantly confused the brake pedal for the gas pedal. We practiced in the alley, where Richard thought I would do the least amount of damage. His instincts were right, I didn't manage to hit anything, but I did run the car into our backyard, driving over the cement foundation that was supposed to be our garage. Time to get a private instructor. He was terrific, except for one thing. He kept wanting me to drive the Eden's expressway every time out. My own thinking was to avoid the expressways at any cost. So I finally asked why he was steering me in this direction every time. He grinned stating, "you'll never know when this will come in handy." Was he ever right. We were off to the suburbs, and that piece of highway would be traveled often.

As the families got larger it was time to get that one family home in the suburbs. My parents at this point had moved out to Skokie, a near north suburb of Chicago. They wanted us to be near them. We had to make a choice as my husband's aunt and uncle wanted us to find a place near them in Old Town near St. Michael's parish on Eugenie and North Park.

Which reminds me of an interesting story Onkel Ben told me on one of our visits when Richard and I were still courting. The story goes like this: In 1911 Onkel Ben arrived in Chicago via Ellis Island. As a young man he had worked at a bank near Osnabrück. As an unmarried young man he was bitten by wanderlust and headed off across the pond for a bit of adventure. He got a job at the Berghoff downtown which at that time was a "gentleman's only" bar. When WWI broke out he was suddenly called to appear in court and after much questioning was let go. Apparently there was some confusion concerning his name. Yet, during WWII he was once again called before the court and asked very similar confusing questions about his name and his background. Again, he was let go. However, this time the judge asked Onkel Ben, "Why don't you change your last name?" You see, he was being confused with a notorious German General Ludendorff and since their names were so similar, this was what brought forth the repeated court appearances. He eventually changed his name to Ben Suden and just lopped off the extra "dorf." No more court appearances.

His sister, Anne followed him to America and immediately began working as an assistant in the dining room at the Stevens Hotel. She loved cooking and would always prepare her meals with heavy brown gravy, the kind I would have to make for Richard. In my family, most of our meals were served *au jus*. Richard later told me the real reason we visited his aunt and uncle so frequently was so that I could learn to master this heavy brown gravy. I also had a taste of my very first Manhattan there Onkel Ben's specialty. At the Berghoff he was known as "martini-Ben."

Richard and I had to make a decision. It was way too expensive to buy a house near his aunt and uncle and so we began looking for a home near my parents in Skokie. My parents had marveled at the beautiful church they belonged to. As it turns out, it was the same church my uncles had labored on when they first came to Chicago. St. Lambert's had been constructed by the firm Schillmoeller and Krofl. Richard and I decided to check it out and we were immediately impressed with the church and its very strong choir.

We sold our two-flat in Chicago. The neighborhood of Skokie was wonderful and with some searching we found a nice one family colonial style home in the parish. As soon as we closed on the house, Richard and I began ripping up carpeting, scraping off paint and wall paper, and getting the house ready for our family. Oma would watch the kids at their home which was about seven blocks from our house. The kids just loved it – in fact, once when we had to pick them up our youngest, Richie said; "Mom, when you're an "Oma" will you cook and bake as good as our "Oma?" This tickled my mother. Little children always tell the truth, even if it hurts, right? On one of these working days at the new house, the doorbell rang and I didn't want to go to the door as I was not dressed for receiving guests. I went anyway, thinking it might be my father.

Wrong. Standing on the front stoop was a large fine looking family. The gentleman greeted me as our neighbor next door. He told us he was a Rabbi at a synagogue just down the street and then introduced his smiling wife Ruth and their four handsome children, one girl and three boys. What a welcome. Richard came out the door covered in dust having just worked on the boiler, whereupon the Rabbi offered any tools that might be of use in our efforts.

They didn't stay long but again offered their assistance. What perfect neighbors! They soon said their goodbyes and the next few days brought more neighbors offering their help and welcoming us to the neighborhood – the Whislers, the Maxons, and the Weils. Once the children moved into the house we met even more neighbors from our block and beyond. When the girls started school, another layer of children and their parents made us feel so very safe and welcome in this community. The children constantly played in each other's yards and oftentimes in the streets. Parents would watch all the kids and yell out to any passing motorist that was speeding and disrupting their play. If a lone car would drive past you would often hear "Slow down!" bellowed from one of the houses on the street. As the girls got older they started babysitting for kids around the neighborhood bringing yet more people into our lives.

In the winter of 1972, we had another boy. Alexander, or Alex, was born and rounded out our family to seven. Our neighbors again, could not do enough for our children while I was at Grant Hospital in Chicago. My mother was a bit hurt when the neighbors stepped in to make dinners and watch the children. She felt a little useless. Once the baby was home though, this changed. There was much ogling, hugging, and grinning over the little boy in his crib. We were finally home.

The children were involved in all the activities that go with school and friends and Richard and I became members of the St Lambert's church choir. We also continued singing with the St. Alphonsus German choir. Our plates were full.

Soccer was the kids' favorite. Not surprising, coming from a soccer playing family. They all played for the Chicago Kickers. First the girls, starting with the Ladies team, then the boys followed as they got old enough to join. What a rat race this turned out to be. Every weekend there were games. The girls at one field, and the boys at a different field. On a few occasions, I even had to fill in for the ladies in their friendly matches as goalie. This was nerve-wracking. Playing with all those young kids. I used my best asset – my voice, and tried to scare away the opposing team by screaming at them. Sometimes this worked, and sometimes not.

The tournaments oftentimes took us out of town, Buffalo Grove, Wheaton, Aurora, Hoffman Estates, Lake Zurich, Lake Villa – boy, was I using the Edens expressway. Now I understood my driving teacher's knowing smile! I couldn't wait until the girls would be old enough to drive themselves as I was truly never a fan of expressway driving.

Richard and I would help out at the clubhouse after the games. The mothers of the players would work endless hours making schnitzel, goulash, bratwurst, pork roasts, hamburgers, hot dogs, potato salad and lots and lots of cake. We would cook not only for our kids' teams but also for all the different Kickers teams. Richard, and some of the other fathers, would take their turns tending bar. There were plenty of noisy, hungry and thirsty players.

One of the girls' coaches was my cousin, Joey Mueller, who took really good care of the team. With the help of his wife, Karin, also a player, Joe trained a very successful bunch of ladies. Our girls all played on the same team; Linda played goalie, Mia defense and Patti was at midfield. For several years, the girls played together, they all seemed to enjoy the game and each other's company tremendously. One year, after a particularly successful season, Joe took the team to Germany to play against a couple of the German teams. This was at first daunting to the girls, playing a German soccer team, but apparently they did very well, or at least they told us they did very well. While in Germany, the girls stayed at the various players' homes in terms of lodging. We were able to return the favor when one of the German teams came to Chicago shortly after. We hosted two girls. What were we thinking? Our house was already full and with these two girls all sharing 1 ½ bathrooms…but we lived through it, with many colorful memories.

As the boys grew older, they too joined the Kicker's youth teams. Rich played defender and Alex played at the forward position. Spending so much time with the other families on the sidelines, celebrating their wins, and consoling their losses, we had a great time and became very close over the years. Thinking back now, I ask myself, how did we do all this? I could not go through that rigor any more.

Apart from soccer taking up a good chunk of our time, we also got involved with our parish activities. As I mentioned earlier, we joined the St. Lambert choir. We divided our Sunday's between choirs – one week at St. Alphonsus, the next at St. Lambert's. The Latin pieces were easy; however, it was the English hymns that proved more beneficial for me. My accent was still very heavy and apparently a source of embarrassment for my children, most especially the boys. On one occasion, my son Rich, asked me not to raise my hand during the school meetings to ask questions. "Just listen to the principal or teacher." he said. I respected his request and reminded myself to hold back even when I had the urge to participate.

In yet another incident, when Alex was a little older, one of his friends called and left a message. This friend later asked Alex if he got the message that he left with the "maid." Alex promptly informed his friend, he did not have a maid, and that was his mother he was speaking to. The choir practices and singing in English would help me with this.

However, I learned that it was not just my accent that caused my boys' embarrassment. One time I presided at lunch recess and brought my son, Alex, who was still quite young. Upon walking into one of the classrooms, one student immediately got out of his chair and shouted, "Heil Hitler." I was stunned. I grabbed my little boy's hand and walked straight home. Now I understood the uneasiness my children felt when I attended the school functions.

I could not even tell my husband about this incident. He would have been furious. I also could not understand that my accent was so heavy when my husband and my other siblings seemed to speak the language so easily. Even to this day, my son Rich ribs me on many occasions, saying, "Mom, I can't believe you've been here 50 years and you still sound like you just got off the boat."

I do what I can. I try the best I can and think that I am speaking the language similar to the natives. However, whenever I meet someone new and I start talking, they begin to smile and immediately ask me where I'm from. I usually say either Chicago or Skokie. And they respond, "That's not what I mean. What country are you from?" Enough said on that topic!

Soon the girls started college. On top of that they all had jobs on the side – sometimes more than one. At one point or other, Patti, Linda, Mia and Rich all worked at Skokie Federal Savings & Loan near our home. This point caught the attention of my youngest, Alex, after I had to say no to a request he made for some special item he had seen on the TV. He asked me, "We're going to be rich soon, aren't we?" I replied, "Why do you say that?" My then-four-year-old pronounced that with his brother and sisters working with all that money that soon we would be rich and could buy anything we wanted!

As you could imagine there was much traffic in our house. This was also noticed by one of our neighbors. She had recently retired and all of her children had moved out of the house. I saw her on the street one day and asked her if she enjoyed the quiet or missed the bustling activity. She turned to me and said, "Whenever, I feel the need for hustle and bustle, I just look out the window at your house and breathe a sigh of relief."

Down the street from us was a synagogue where our neighbor officiated. On Fridays at sundown and during the days on Saturdays we would see the rabbi and his family walking to services. They were all so very well dressed and dignified. We quickly stopped mowing our lawns on their Sabbath, respecting their holy day. We didn't wish to offend. No one ever said our lawn was too long if we missed cutting it every once in a while.

Although we lived in a community where many of our neighbors were not Catholic, we never felt uncomfortable in pursuing our own religion or traditions. I remember at Christmas, our Catholic neighbors, the Kneips, the Noonans, the Hylands and our kids would go around caroling. Afterwards Marge Noonan would have us all over at her place for hot chocolate and donuts in front of a warm and crackling fireplace. The kids loved it, almost as much as the grown-ups.

It was around that time we started a Christ Kindle market at St. Lambert's. This usually took place around St. Nicklaus Day. All the ladies of the parish took part either baking or creating beautiful homemade goods including mittens, scarves, ornaments, holiday decorations and lovely Irish sweaters. Margret and Josef Soehn, with a handful of loyal helpers, made fancy cookie houses every year – somewhere between 30 and 40 such houses – with a replica of a famous or not-so-famous church as their centerpiece each year. Let me see if I remember them all – St. Lambert's church, of course; St. Peter's in Skokie, St. Mary's in Evanston; St. Pasqual in Chicago, in honor of our Cardinal George; St. Alphonsus; Holy Name Cathedral, St. Stephan's, in Vienna; St. Basil in Moscow – that's all I remember. For the local churches, Josef would drive around and take pictures to inspire us. For the others, we relied on photos from travel brochures and pictures we'd seen and also much from memories we had had of visiting these faraway churches.

This was a concerted effort of all St. Lambert parishioners. Josef did all the hard work building the frames. The ladies would decorate the walls with cookies, candies and frostings. The parishioners would generously donate all the ingredients. After each mass leading up to the Christ Kindle Market, the ladies would collect boxes and bags of cookies and candies and frosting to build all of the houses.

It was also during this time that I was working at Delicatessen Mayer in Chicago. I had often spoken about these cookie houses to the owners, Klaus and Renate Koetke. They participated in a similar Christ Kindle market in Lincoln Square right at the intersection of Lincoln Avenue and Giddings. One year, they asked if we would like to sell our St. Lambert cookie houses at their market. It was just about the coldest winter that year, but we sold each and every one of those houses – it was quite a success.

That following year, Renate asked me if I would make a cookie house for the display window during the holiday season. So we created a Bavarian chalet, covered with Christmas cookies and frosting that sat in the window from the beginning of that Christmas season until New Year's. It was not long after this that the city of Chicago introduced the Christ Kindle Market to its citizens. Located at the Daley Center, German artisans display and sell their crafts during the holiday season. This has become a regular tradition in Chicago – still going strong from Thanksgiving until December 24. Every time we go there, it brings me back to the days of my youth in Rothenburg.

Chapter 6

The Happy Wanderers

One year when Alex was either four or five and I think Patti might have been Miss Kickers, my mother-in-law and Richard's sister, Elizabeth, came to visit from Germany. Since they were farmers, they wanted to see our countryside. We took them to Bell's Apple Orchard near Lake Zurich. We all had a field day, climbing trees and filling bushels and bushels of apples. On the way back, there was an extremely long traffic back-up on Golf Road. Many of the drivers had gotten out of their cars and began walking east toward Skokie Boulevard. We did the same. As we got closer, we could see men with rifles standing atop the then Hilton hotel. There were security men everywhere. Just as we reached the curb at Skokie Boulevard and Golf, a caravan of black limousines came out of the hotel's driveway, zooming by just in front of us. A face appeared out of one of those windows. It was President Ford, waving to us. Alex made a quick salute and the President smiled in return. My mother-in-law was so surprised and stated, in German, of course: "All my life, I've never seen any of our leaders so close up as I've just seen your President. I can't wait to tell my neighbors back home."

As if that wasn't enough excitement. The next day she wanted to see the famous John Hancock building downtown. I drove her there and Alex accompanied us. On the northwest corner of Michigan and Delaware I stopped to let her and my son Alex out while I tried to find a parking space. You know how that goes, in Chicago. Well, no sooner had I closed the door behind them, when I heard a sharp banging on my car. Startled I looked up to see a gruff Chicago policeman shouting at me telling me, "Hey Lady, you can't park here."

I tried to explain to him that I only stopped to let out my mother-in-law, who was visiting from Germany, as she had difficulty walking far. He listened to me and then replied apologetically, "Well alright, I'll keep an eye on them." And he did. What a lasting image he left on my mother-in-law of Chicago – this officer of the law – first rough and gruff and then so patient and helpful.

Going back to the Ms. Kickers thing. As I mentioned before, Patti had been crowned Ms. Kickers around the same time and that year she had also been named Ms. Soccer at the Sport, Funk and Presse Ball, an annual formal dance sponsored by all the local amateur soccer teams. What this meant, was that besides representing German soccer teams at various functions, she would be riding on a float during the annual Von Steuben Parade along with her court made up of the various soccer queens representing their clubs. The Steuben parade got its name from General Von Steuben, a Prussian General who aided General George Washington during the revolutionary war. My mother-in-law, Sudendorf's mum, joined us at the parade and just delighted herself with all this über activity in our town. She lived in such a small village in Germany all her life. She had crossed the pond, roamed around the large and busy city of Chicago all while in her early 80's. She definitely held bragging rights back home.

A few years later, before Alex started school and Patti started college the seven of us took what would incredibly be our last family vacation together. We were off to the wild west. Finally! We had wanted to make this trip for many years, but for one reason or another we were never able to pull it off. My sister Perpetua, her husband, Norbert and their children, Michael, Tina and Kenny as well as my younger brother Adi, his wife, Wallie and their little girl, Cindy also wanted to join in the fun. They however, wanted to go a bit rough and tumble and make a camping trip out of this adventure. Everybody was for this idea except me. I had my fill of "roughing it." All the time we were fleeing in the covered wagon during the war ended any desire I had to "camp out."

My family rallied around me and we decided to travel by car and stay at hotels, while my sister and brother and their families vacationed via campers and tents. Destination: Colorado. All three families were to meet up in Rapid City, South Dakota in two days and my brood set out for our first stop, Iowa City. Leaving Chicago, we first had to make our way through the vast industrial landscape before our world opened up to the welcoming open plains filled with farmland and big skies. It was at this point I started to relax.

Before you knew it we were upon the mighty Mississippi. We all had to get out of the car and marvel at its great size and beauty. Trying to think what those first settlers thought when they first encountered this awesome river. Well, these bridges certainly made the crossing easier for us! We then pressed on through miles and miles of gold and green corn fields as we drove toward our destination.

We stayed at a Holidome in Iowa City and the children couldn't wait to jump into the pool. We couldn't get them out no matter how hard we tried or what food we bribed them with. The next morning we headed a bit north to South Dakota, first through Sioux City, then along the famous Missouri, and finally westward through endless grassland, seeming to grow as far as the eye could see. There was nothing but flat green grass and above us a huge perfect blue sky. There were no farms, no cattle, not a single soul in sight. It appeared we were the only travelers on this road some-where between heaven and earth.

The sheer open space around us made you feel both insignifi-cant and empowered. I could only imagine how astronauts might feel –peering at these wide, vast, empty spaces. In the distance we could see a sign. We hoped for some indication of either a hotel or a spot to eat but all we saw was "Wall Drugs." This same sign we saw over and over again on this leg of our journey as if "Wall Drug" owned all this land. It was confusing. Finally, a lone car approached from the other side. I don't know how long we had driven without seeing any other person's but it had to be signifi-cant if this is a memory I still hold after all these years.

After, what seemed like hours, our view changed to a hilly grass covered vista. The first herd of cattle was visible in the distance, though still no farm houses or silos. Were these cattle wild or were they buffalos? Or was the rancher so rich he tended his cattle via helicopter? All this open land could not possibly belong to one man? How did the early settlers manage this open terrain? No trees could be seen for any type of shelter, and with all those harsh winters with only their wagons for protection. These were all the questions going through my head. I imagined their travels west and compared them to my own memories of our flight west in Europe during the war. Here we were traveling for pleasure and in comfort. And we knew our final destination.

We started singing…. our usual pastime for car journeys short or long. This time our repertoire mostly included songs from the heartland and the wild west. It was never boring, no matter how long the trip. And of course there were always *Schnitchen* (small sandwiches) on hand in case the crew got hungry.

Finally, we saw not only cattle grazing, but buffalo and beautiful green pastures. This scenery changed quickly into bumpy outcrops – not pointy, but more rounded as though they had been molded that way. So different from the mountains I remembered in Europe. This, I learned later, was the Badlands. I was so pleased that Richard and Patti did all the driving as this allowed me to revel in the sights flying past us. I also hate driving!

As we drove further, we entered a deep, dark, green forest. We began to see more signs of civilization, which was perfect as the kids were starting to get antsy. We had arrived in Rapid City, South Dakota. The young ones especially were squirming to get checked in the hotel so that they could dive into the indoor pool at the Holidome. This was where we were to rendezvous with my siblings and their families. They had traveled by way of campgrounds and when we met up, all of the cousins immediately donned bathing suits and joined our crew in the indoor pool. When the pool closed, everyone piled into our room to catch up on each other's adventures and this lasted into the wee hours of the night.

In the morning, we split up on our outing to the Black Hills. The children all opted for the "fun-mobile" the name they gave the outfitted van my brother-in-law had rented for the trip. We, older folks were relegated to the more subdued mode of transportation. The next leg of our journey took us through some very treacherous and scary roads with steep drop offs at almost every turn. We finally, made it to the place where our President's faces were etched into the mountain. I was completely awed. All of the cousins gathered and created a human pyramid – something they would do quite frequently when they were so inspired and had enough kids together. I could never understand how this particular tradition got started, but my photo collection includes quite a few of these poses.

After all the pictures were snapped there was a call for some provisions. This is one area we were always prepared for. My sister-in-law, Wallie had brought an entire Hungarian salami which we devoured on this impromptu picnic in the forest. Although the benches were still wet from the previous night's rain, it didn't stop us from sitting our happy selves upon them as we dined al fresco. There was no sound but for the winds soaring through the treetops, whispering to each other. It felt as if you were in an old historic church – it had that same sound. It was around this time that I truly felt I belonged in this country. I no longer felt like a foreigner, but instead, an American. Strange, isn't it? After a stroll through this amazing site, we moved onward to try to find "Where the Buffalos roamed..." We quickly spotted them. They were not shy. They grazed right near us. This was also amazing to me, that this country would save these magnificent animals.

Off in the distance were some beautiful purple flowers. Wallie kept marveling at them. As we were driving, Richard abruptly stopped the car near a meadow with the buffalos and stopped to pluck some for her. He returned to the car and thrust his hand forward –"Here, Wallie, here are your 'flowers.'" They turned out to be thistles and everyone roared.

The next morning we again went our separate ways. The campers went further west to explore Yellowstone Park. Our family journeyed south to Colorado as we were more pressed for time. The landscape toward Cheyenne, Wyoming again changed dramatically. It was vast and wide and deserted and here and there dotted with buttes – larger and smaller ones. Once again, there was very little traffic on this leg of our journey. As the sun set and the sky turned purplish red and took on an eerie, ghostlike appearance. I had to wonder how you could find all these changing landscapes within one country.

Finally, we entered into Colorado driving through Denver, Estes Park, and then Vail. The scenery again, was so different. It reminded me so much of the Alps which immediately put me at ease. Driving through these serpentine roads was treacherous to be sure. Richard and Patti once again took the wheel during this leg of the journey which held quite a few white-knuckled twists and turns. Once again, I was thrilled not to have had been asked to take the wheel. Whew!

Once this harrowing ride was behind us, we were finally able to relax as Vail opened up before us. The surrounding hills were green and majestic with wild flowers growing everywhere. A shallow creek splashed downhill into the town seeming to evade the large boulders in its path. I felt like a child again, wanting to jump from stone to stone as I watched my children teetering on these rocks just itching to fall into the water. The stately homes sitting on the hillside also appeared to teeter on the pillars that made up their foundations. They were beautiful... as was the little church we visited that Sunday. Its simplicity perfectly fit into this landscape. Up front, behind the altar, rather than stained glass, was a huge window that framed the splendor of nature peering in from the outdoors. You could hear the gurgling of the little creek that ran alongside. You didn't even need inspiring words or music. Here I truly felt transported to another world.

Later, we all took a walk up the hill and through the meadows near a golf course where we were told President Ford had a chalet. From what we could see from the path was simply lovely. We also took a tram up to the top of the ski lift and were rewarded with a gorgeous view of the town below. Vail had definitely been the highlight of the trip for me. After leaving Vail, we took a trip along the continental divide. At one point we all got out of the car, to venture out until I spied a sign that said "watch out for wildlife." That's all I needed – and I hurried the kids back into the car and we quickly made our "escape."

We were now on our journey back toward home. Through Denver and then east through Nebraska, It was as if we were in the middle of a wild west movie – big open prairies with tumble weed being blown everywhere. All that was missing were the cowboys on horseback chasing a young calf that might have strayed from the herd. As we went on we could see in the distant horizon a storm was brewing. The tumbleweeds began to roll fiercely about us. Then it started pouring. Hard. Lightening came closer and closer and slashed brighter and with greater fury. There was nowhere for us to take cover. We stopped singing. We were all pretty scared. To take our minds off our fears, we started counting between lightening strikes and the ensuing rolls of thunder. I had never experienced such a violent showing of nature before this. It remains vivid in my memory to this day. After what seemed the longest day, the weather finally became tame and we made the rest of the return home in calm surroundings. It was the vacation I'll never forget!

Chapter 7

The Kids Grow Up – Life Changes

As the school year started in 1979, my mother passed away. She was the first of my immediate family to die and with her passing, many of our family traditions ended. No longer would we smell the fragrant aromas coming from the house when our family pulled up into their driveway. The long standing tradition of Christmas Eve would no longer take place at my parents' house with all the children and grandchildren. The heart of this larger family had stopped beating.

My father especially was devastated. We invited my father to stay with us after her passing and he did – for one night. After which he informed Richard and I that although he appreciated our generous invitation, he wanted to have the option of going to his own home, especially when things got a bit noisy at our house. While he loved spending time with the children, when he had his fill, he could always escape back to his home. We of course honored his wishes.

I think that helped him. Because my family lived within walking distance of his home, he could walk to our house daily joining us for supper. Before the children returned from school he would have arrived and would have stood waiting for them at the front door. He would stay for dinner and then insisted on walking home on his own. It was ok in the summer time, however, in the winter, when it would get dark early, one of us would drive him to his house. The kids usually volunteered for this chore as they were all just getting their driver's licenses and wanted a chance to drive on their own. This worked out just fine as I was not a big fan of driving – I was always on pins and needles whenever I got behind the wheel of a car.

My parents had always had a large network mostly made up of their brothers, sisters, many cousins and extended families. They would gather each Saturday evening to play cards, reminisce and share a homemade meal together. Living in and around the Chicago area they all seemed to get along well. What better company and support could you ask for and they provided this for my father especially after he lost his wife. He still wasn't the same.

After my mother passed away he insisted on returning to his birthplace. He wanted to see his homeland once more. Maybe he felt time was running out on him too. Even though he and my mom had visited Germany and Austria together several times visiting relatives, he had never returned to his birthplace, Rumania. His niece, Nina and her family from Austria were planning a similar trip and he was delighted to accompany them. He flew to Vienna and they drove from Austria to Rumania along the Danube River. He loved it. One of the highlights he shared with us upon returning to Chicago was his therapeutic swim in the Black Sea and since he had a bad back and knees, he treated himself to these medicinal waters regularly. He had asked me to accompany him but I couldn't. I had just started a new job so taking this time off would be near impossible. I still regret this.

Another loss to our extended family was felt by my youngest brother Al. He and his wife Gail had just welcomed their fourth child, Martina to their family. She was just an infant and had two older brothers, Matt and Michael John and a sister, Melanie. The tiny little *Mädelein* died of sudden infant death syndrome just a few short months with us. It was a frigid snowy day in January, 1980 when Richard, my father and I piled into the car and headed north to Crystal Lake. As we started making our way entering the Edens expressway, the car began to slip and slide and career out of control. We all struggled with our dilemma and in the end we decided to return to our homes and missed her funeral. I deeply regret this moment as well. Knowing how hurt and lost my brother and his wife must have felt, they needed as much comfort and support as they could get and we let the weather get in the way.

A few years later, our oldest daughter, Patti graduated from Loyola University Law School. This was our first law school graduate in the family and my father wanted to honor this occasion by taking us all out to dinner at a restaurant in Old Town. I believe it was called "The Chicago Bar Association" and at the conclusion of the meal, my father promptly pulled out his checkbook and began writing a check for the whole shebang. Unfortunately, the restaurant would not accept personal checks. This just goes to show you how often my father, or our family for that matter, actually went out for dinner. Dinners for us were almost exclusively a home cooked affair. More on that later.

After we got home, my father couldn't resist the temptation to tease Patti saying, "I don't know why you waste your time studying to become a lawyer, and a criminal lawyer at that, why don't you learn to cook like women should and find yourself a husband!" This topic would provide constant bickering between the two, almost as if they were adversaries in their own courtroom.

Too bad he couldn't have seen her at work at the Cook County State's Attorney's office – he would have loved it!

Linda, the second oldest had attended Loyola as an undergraduate and during one semester she chose to take her studies in Rome. How romantic! Her major was business but I wonder how much "business" she actually was studying in Italy! Shortly upon her return, a dark, young, handsome Italian speaking man visited us. The women in the household were intrigued, I think – the men – not so much. My husband was suspicious, my sons outright rude at times. I suppose they were just being protective. We all however breathed a sigh of relief when he decided to return to his Italian homeland.

Unfortunately, my father became sick not long after. My sister and brothers and their families would visit him often at Augustana Hospital on Lincoln Avenue. After our many visits we would gather at *Zum Deutchen Eck.* It's a shame neither one of these places is there anymore. These places were full of memories for us – some wonderful and some much more sobering.

Just before Thanksgiving of that year they told us my father could no longer live on his own, and that we should make some arrangements. We decided he would stay either at my sister Pat's or at my house. The doctors thought it might be easier for him to stay at Pat's since she had less people at home. We were encouraged by this news, even though to us our father did not look that well. The next day we received a call from the hospital; Opa had died. At his funeral all of his grandsons served as his pall bearers – those young men all dutifully performed their duty crying throughout.

It was also around this time that Patti, Linda and Mia decided to move out of the house and find an apartment in town. They would leave the family nest and like many of their generation would exercise their independence by going out on their own. This was so different from my own experience where a young person would remain in the family home until he or she got married. I hated this new idea but it was something I had to get used to.

Each of my children would venture out to faraway places quite a bit before any of them got married – and some I'm still waiting to walk down the aisle….. Patti lived in Texas, Oklahoma and South Carolina. Linda lived In London for quite a time. Mia moved out to Colorado and Alex moved to Phoenix, Arizona. Only Richard, our oldest son remained close to us and still does to this day. This I always appreciated.

Patti was the first one to go. One day, shortly after graduating Loyola University as an undergraduate, she announced to us all during dinner that she was moving down to Dallas, Texas. At the time, all I knew about Dallas was that one of our Presidents, John F. Kennedy had been assassinated there. I was not thrilled to hear this news. She ended up staying there for a few years and then moved to Oklahoma City – a place I knew even less about. She moved back to Chicago shortly thereafter to attend law school, which I wrote about earlier and then worked as a prosecutor with the Cook County office for several years. She later moved to Columbia, South Carolina, and it was during her time there I learned so much of the history and people of the South with their gentile and welcoming manner. Patti is currently back in Chicago. For how long, I cannot say. Right now she lives with me and is helping me write this memoir so I will leave it at that.

Linda traveled the world. We already spoke about her Italian adventures, but additionally, her various positions within financial institutions enabled her to travel to Spain, Italy, Sweden, France, and finally landed her in London, England. Through her position with Fidelity Investments which she began here, in Chicago, she was able to move overseas to a place called Kensington, in London. The family took full advantage of this assignment and we would visit her and Tim (more on that later) often using this as a springboard to other European destinations. She also worked in Germany and Luxemburg with her work. What an adventure! But she ended up coming back to Chicago too – see?

Mia started at DePaul majoring in chemistry and sometime after graduating she moved out to Colorado with her job at Gates. The kids all visited with her in Denver although I never was able to make it. What a shame! I loved Colorado from that first time we had visited. While she was living out there she decided she also wanted to go into law and started studying patent law. It was also during this time, she met and married Rick and after the two of them celebrated their union at St. Alphonsus – a recurring theme – they headed back to Colorado. It was just a matter of time before they too returned to the Chicago area. After moving about the northern suburbs for what seemed like every other year, they finally settled in Park Ridge. They now have three children, Olivia, Julia and Lukas, the grandchildren, I referred to earlier in this book, you remember, the one's I told these bed-time stories to. Right now they too live right around the corner. Are you seeing a pattern here?

Richard Jr. never had quite the same level of wanderlust. Although he would travel – he was the first of us to see the Berlin wall which was then still standing (he also had his camera taken away from him by the East German police who would require his teacher to intervene on his behalf to get the apparatus back!) he was happiest with his entourage in Skokie. We oftentimes kidded him about being the "Mayor" of Skokie. He always knew of the latest happenings here – having periodically worked at both Principal's and the Village Inn, he knew the comings and goings, ins and outs of all the residents. You could always count on him to give us the latest updates of some of Skokie's more colorful characters. He also loved *Wurst*; so much so that when he was a little boy; maybe six or seven, he once commandeered a whole salami I had brought home from Mayer's delicatessen and hid it under his bed. I found it later that day when I noticed his bed sheets were awry. You'd think I never fed that boy! Richard Jr., loves my cooking. You will find him on any given Sunday – unless we're eating at one of the other girl's homes, at my house for a good home cooked meal. Some things never change – and I'm happy for that!

Alexander Bernhard was our youngest. He was the long awaited brother to Rich, second son to my husband, and "cuddly plaything" for our girls. They all mothered him. They couldn't help it. As the youngest, he was probably spoiled. At least that's what the older kids always chided me about. "The boys always get away with everything," they would say. But they too, spoiled him. As he grew up he always made the kids laugh and laughed at himself. He rounded out the family perfectly. Alex's adventures took him from the family home to Tempe, Arizona where he would join his friend, Aaron to start his career. As you can see, all of our children had a bit of the *wanderlust*.

Chapter 8

Passings

It was right during the time that Mia had returned from Colorado to Chicago to take the bar and was living with us that Richard became very ill. He had lung cancer the doctor's informed us. He was in the hospital about a week. They told us there really was no hope. I had had an inkling. Just a few days before, Linda and I had gone to the hospital to see him and Richard was feverish. Linda stood in the doorway crying, and when I approached Richard he asked who I had brought with to visit. I asked him if he meant Linda, and he said no – rather the man in the black coat that stood behind me. He must have been delirious. Or else he was having some kind of premonition.

Not long after he was admitted we were called to a meeting with his doctors who told us there was really nothing they could do. Did Richard know already? Is that why he saw the man in the black coat? I really will never know. Richard decided he wanted to die at home and so we made arrangement for our home to be prepared especially for him. We contacted hospice care who provided a bed, oxygen, and a visiting nurse who came on a regular basis to make certain Richard was getting the right amount of morphine so that it wouldn't be that painful for him.

I called my work at Mayer's Delicatessen, to request the time off to stay at home and they completely understood and told me to take whatever time I needed. The visitors started coming on a regular basis. The first of which were Rabbi and Mrs. Montrose, our neighbors. The priests from our parish also came regularly. Family, friends, his brother Joe came to visit almost every day. This seemed to calm him – especially the visits from his brother. His old friends from Kolping, Alois and Albert and his wife, Leni came and our visits almost always included a cup of tea with Stroh Rum. Funny, the things you remember. We all tried to spend as much quality time with him as we could. You could tell however, that the end was not long off.

One time, I had gone down to make tea and when I returned he was not in his bed. Mia, who was in the room across the hall, involved in her studies, had no idea where he was. I was about to call the hospital when I smelled smoke – cigarette smoke specifically – coming from the bathroom. I knocked on the door with no answer. But I could hear him shuffling around. Finally, after several moments he emerged, very proud of himself. I couldn't believe it! I thought about every time I had struggled with him to get him from the bed to the bathroom and here he had made this trip all by himself for a cigarette!

That night, he was especially restless. I sat on his favorite grandfather's chair which the boys had moved upstairs for him. He had not used it now for a while and so I sat there, curled up on a sheet. He couldn't speak at that point anymore but at times he would sit straight up and stare at me as if he was looking right through me. Towards morning, his breathing was laboring, gargling. I told Mia to get a hold of the rest of the kids and to call our pastor.

All of the children arrived one by one. As Richard took his last breath we were all around him upstairs. Everyone was silent. Just sitting there. Searching for words. Yet no sounds came. It was a moment frozen in time. There was something so powerful about being all together at this sad yet awesome moment. I thought of all the soldiers who lay dying so far from home yearning for the touch or sound of their loved ones. In this way, we were so very fortunate to be present at his final moment.

At the wake at Haben's funeral home in Skokie, our German choir again assembled to sing a final farewell. The choir director, Alfred Schoepko, gave a moving speech – not really a eulogy, but a tome, part scripture, part poem, part memoir that moved all of us. He gave each of the children a copy and we have them still. The choir sang beautifully. I remember Tim and Rick standing ram rod straight behind me almost as guards, as all of us greeted our many friends and family. There were so many people who came to the wake and funeral. We were grateful for all of the outpouring of love and kindness that day and the days and weeks that followed.

That following year was strange and filled with much upheaval. It seemed everyone was moving out of the house. Mia and Rick were returning to Colorado. Linda and Patti were long out of the house. Richie had moved into an apartment with friends and Alex was just finishing up his internship with a mortgage lending company and would soon be heading out to Arizona with this new job. I did not like any of this. I would soon be alone in this big four bedroom house. This did not sit well. I didn't want to be alone dwelling on the sorrow. So going back to work was welcomed. During that following year, the children would come home for Sunday dinner every weekend. This helped but at night I would contemplate my situation and for the first time I thought about selling the family house. All the children were happy in their individual situations so a condo sounded very practical to me.

There was some wonderful news that came during this turbulent time for me. Mia and Rick returned from Colorado and had their first baby girl – Olivia. She was an angel that really saved us during this very sad and lonely time. So as a family, we did bounce back at least for a while.

That fall, my brother Anthony passed away. He had, however, been fortunate to have been able to attend his oldest son, Jim and Heather's wedding just that summer before. The wedding was in August and just a few months later he would die. How very sad – he was in his early 50's. In one year I had lost my husband and then my brother. He was the first of our siblings to go. The rest of us, Pat, Adi, Al and I decided we wanted to return to Wettringen before too much time passed. And so we did.

Adi had received an invitation from Hannelore, an old classmate in Wettringen to attend a reunion. We made our plans and flew to Munich, where Al rented a van and all of us, including Adi's wife, Wallie, packed ourselves into the car and began our journey back through our childhood. First through Dingolfing, (they make BMW's there) where we looked up our Tante Lisbeth and Onkel Benno and their son, Benno. They were wonderfully gracious and we talk about their hospitality to this day. We visited our Onkel Carl and Tante Ida in Hagelstadt near Regensburg, and the whole clan of relatives who lived around the area. After a detour through Neuschwanstein (the inspiration for the Disney castle), we took the *Romantische Strasse* north to Rothenburg and then onto Wettringen. We roamed around in our old stomping grounds. We stayed in Rothenburg at the *Altfrankische Weinstube*. How beautiful and romantic!

Entering Wettringen we remarked at all of our old landmarks. As we neared the center of town we walked into the *Gasthaus zur*

Post which is where some of the other reunion folks were staying. We didn't recognize any of them. Then again, we were children when we left, but after introductions were made, we smiled and fell easily into conversation.

It was bittersweet learning that our home had been demolished and in its place was a new kindergarten structure. We had learned the Herr Strecker, had had no children so he had bequeathed his farm to the village. This was convenient to the middle of town. In the afternoon, there was a parade to the festival tent where we visited with almost everyone from the village. Guest choirs were invited which made for some fierce competition among the choirs and a very loud and lively atmosphere. People came to our table and introduced themselves. We saw old friends and made new ones.

The next day we walked all of the paths we had traversed those many years ago. Pat's meadows, the boys' hills, and we all told stories, remembering all who lived there and all our adventures. We had one of the best times. So much so, we made a pact to do this more often. Our children were grown and could take care of themselves. We would travel. This sounded like a fine idea and although some of us have been able to return with our children, unfortunately, we're still, as of this writing, waiting to band together for another "sibling adventure."

Chapter 9

Losing Alex

It was 1997 and another Easter season was upon us. This included choir practices, extra Holy Week services and finally, a gathering at the house to have our anticipated Easter meal. The only one missing was Alex, who couldn't make it home from Arizona. He had just started working there that past February and couldn't get the time off. I understood, but it nevertheless put a damper on the celebrations. These holiday gatherings were always much fun and brought forth much laughter and over-excited conversation which filled the day. Of course, good food and wine was always the requisite. If the day was nice enough, we would have these banquets on the screened porch – one of our favorite "dining" spots. After lunch we would oftentimes have an Easter egg hunt in the backyard and any of the cousins, aunts and uncles who came to visit would participate.

Very early the next Monday morning, the doorbell rang. I was just in my robe heading downstairs to make some coffee. Who could this be so early? Maybe one of the kids had left something important behind? I looked out the bay window to make certain it wasn't a stranger. It was. Two police officers, a male and a female stood out on the front stoop. The first thought that entered my mind was hoping that no one was in an accident.

I opened the door and both asked very politely if I was Mrs. Sudendorf and if they could come in. They also asked me if anyone else was home. This gave me the first suspicion that something wasn't right – someone was hurt. After I told them I was alone, they didn't want to come forward right away and asked me if I could call a family member to come over. Now I feared it was one of the children. They called Rich, who lived the closest and he was here in no time. While we waited for him, I was pressing the officers for more information. First they asked me if I had a son who lived in Tempe, Arizona. I told them, yes and asked them how bad is it? I asked just as Rich came in the house. They took a long pause before answering and I could feel my voice failing me. I held on to Rich and everything seemed to stop around me.

The officer told Rich that Alex had been riding home on a bicycle and a young lady had hit him with her car. She had been driving under the influence. Alex died in the hospital. He was 25 years old. The poor kid had to die all alone, in a faraway place with none of us there. We couldn't even close his eyes at the end. I was so grateful to Rich. He had been the last one to drive down with him just a few months earlier.

Each of the girls came home. One by one they came through the door and we stared and held each other. We were in disbelief. We sobbed uncontrollably. How could this happen? Hadn't we lost so much already? Even the trials of going through the war could not have been more devastating. How would we go on?

The doorbell rang and there stood the Rabbi from next door. How did he know we needed help at this moment? Shortly thereafter, my two brothers, Adi and Al walked through the door.

Their faces mirrored the sadness and heartbreak of my own. They came and gave us so much comfort with their words and really by just being there. I will never forget that feeling of protection. They could not have come at a more necessary time. How they came so quickly, my brother Al from Crystal Lake, I will never know. Reflecting back, however, it was a great comfort to have family, friends and neighbors at this most devastating and pivotal point in my life.

The children made all the calls to family and to the church. Our pastor, Father Luszak came immediately, bringing a large chocolate chip cookie. This seemed odd to me at first since this was more of a Jewish custom, so I had believed, but it was a welcome gesture. He remained with us for quite some time sharing a story he had of his sister who had also perished in an auto accident. I had changed clothes finally as more of our family and friends began coming to the house. Arrangements had to be made. I would need a clearer head. I had to go on. The other children, they needed me.

Each of the children took control of the arrangements that came with preparing for the funeral. They all seemed controlled and poised at the wake. When they led us to the casket, I couldn't believe how good Alex looked... as if he were just sleeping. It wasn't until I caressed his head that I lost my composure and broke down weeping for him. I couldn't still believe it. We wanted to have a closed casket and so this was the only time I would have this moment. The children and I regained our composure and stood in our places greeting the hundreds of family, friends, and associates who came to the wake – it was standing room only. Each of the choirs I belonged to sang at the wake – the German choir and the St. Lambert's choir. It was incredibly moving and I think everyone, no matter how well they might have known Alex or not, got a lump in their throat.

At one point I remember my son-in-law Rick taking me aside for a drink of water and some air. There was a crush of people inside. As we returned, there was this man kneeling on the floor in front of Alex's coffin with his head bowed deep in prayer. He came to me and my daughter introduced him as her then boss- Dick Devine. He had seemed so humbled. It was not what I had expected from a politician. Someone I had never met.

When we said goodbye to the last of the well-wishers, reality set in. All of the consolations from our friends, though appreciated, would soon end, and we would be alone, without Alex. We held on to each other and Rick took me aside and insisted on taking me home in his car. On our way home we picked up little Olivia who was about nine months old. She had stayed at one of their friends – the Hanleys. At first, I didn't see the significance of the detour but then he suggested we have Olivia stay with me at my house. What a fine idea that was. She needed all of our attention that night and didn't allow us time to linger on this tragedy. Linda had also spent the night and we had Olivia sleep between us. We both feared we would squish this tiny baby and so neither of us slept very well. I will always be grateful for this gesture. For keeping this angel with us truly helped me get through this night.

The day of the funeral all the children gathered at the house. We first went to the funeral home and then onto St. Lambert's for Alex's last mass. It was all very formal, I'm sure, but for me, I was mostly in a fog. I do remember the beautiful and heartbreaking psalm, *Jerusalem, Jerusalem*, which the St. Lambert's traditional choir and children's choir sang. At the cemetery itself, with all the children, family and friends about it was hard to keep my emotions in check. Even afterwards at our home, when everyone came after the funeral procession, I struggled to keep it together. But with all of the commotion of the day, the mourners staying at our home it was also helpful in pushing the reality of it all further away.

Some days later, looking through the registry with all of those names, some I knew, most I did not. But, I do remember the first name on the top was Father Murtaugh, our retired pastor of St. Lambert's who had come to pay his respects. This comforted me greatly.

It was good that the children got time off from work. This would have been too hard to bear alone. The following days, we all sort of drifted. No one wanted to go to bed. No one wanted to eat. We all sort of sat around. No one wanting to break the bond that was just holding us there.

The following Sunday, the Rabbi came to our door once more. He informed us he would bring dinner to us as soon as his wife Ruth had finished. He would not take "no" for an answer. We set the table and just then the doorbell rang and there stood the Rabbi with a steaming pot of chicken soup. He told us he would return in a moment with the rest. We had barely finished the soup when he returned with chicken, rice and broccoli. I couldn't believe it. It seemed to me as if a page had been lifted from the Bible in this gesture. My grandmother used to say, your neighbors are your first responders, so treat them well.

This set the stage for the following days. Every evening thereafter someone, many of them my children's friends, brought food for the family. I don't think I cooked for two weeks afterward. It's kind of sad though, to think you have to wait until death to realize how many friends you have.

Linda had taken a leave of absence from work, which was a blessing as the rest of the crew had to return to work. It was time to move out of the house. I could no longer stay in this big, empty four-bedroom house. We were able to sell the house on our own and I had to move the furniture into storage as I had not yet found a place to live. Alex's friends all came to help wrap and move the furniture. In the meantime, at their invitation, I moved in with Mia and Rick in Mt. Prospect. There was little Olivia to cuddle whenever I came home from work. This was so necessary in keeping my mind off the tragedy of losing Alex.

It was later that year, in October, I believe, we found some lovely condos in downtown Skokie. The kids liked it as well as it was centrally located to all of them. So we signed on. The bad thing about moving though is not knowing who your new neighbors might be. It would be great if you could bring your good neighbors with you, however, since this is not possible, I moved not so far away, where everything was still somewhat familiar and my new neighbors turned out to be just fine.

Chapter 10

The Family Grows

I wasn't the only one in the family pulling up stakes. It was about this same time that Linda received an offer from her job to move to London, England. This was great news for the whole family. Not that Linda was leaving us, but rather this opportunity would give us all the benefit of visiting Europe more often and at this time it was more appreciated than ever. Before she left for England, she had met Tim and they enjoyed an international courtship which finally brought them back home to Chicago to marry at St. Alphonsus church in January of 1998. This was, of course the same church Richard and I were married in back in 1957 and the church Maria and Rick were married in back in 1993. The St. Lambert's children's choir filled the church with beautiful hymns, including two of my favorites *Ave Maria* and *Panis Angelicus*.

It was an unseasonably warm but rainy January day so Linda didn't even wear a coat. She had brought her wedding gown all the way from London – very chic, and Linda was apparently too much in love to worry about getting it wet! But that is love, isn't it? The reception itself was held at Salvatore's – very elegant.

Mia was pregnant again with their second, little Olivia was the flower girl and was the most serious, little flower girl you ever saw walk down the aisle, and even though we all felt Alex missing, we were able to enjoy ourselves and celebrate this happy occasion. Weddings bring great joy and this one was no exception.

Around Easter of that year, the Olsons welcomed a new family member – baby Julia and boy, did she have a pair of lungs. No wonder she has such a powerful singing voice now. When she was only six months old or maybe even a year, and when Olivia was maybe two, the Olsons flew off to London to visit Linda and Tim. How many youngsters can boast that at such a tender age? When Julia was just a wee baby she would cuddle on my shoulder and hum the first two measures of the lullaby of *Schlaf, Kindlein, Schlaf,* in short staccato notes. Then she would stop, waiting for me to chime in. If I didn't, she'd start all over again. It was amazing, listening to these first musical accomplishments. Well done! I guess I needed to be reminded of the small wonders that children can unfold. We always seem so very busy, but these moments with my grandchildren, let me slow down and marvel at their every accomplishment.

With an open invitation from the Ransfords to come and visit often, I took them up on their offer and flew to London. This was the first time I had flown anywhere solo and although I was a little intimidated at first – I knew they spoke English there so how hard could that be? As I walked through Heathrow, I spotted a sign with my name on it. Linda had informed me of this procedure and so I promptly followed the gentleman. He introduced himself as Richard and escorted me to a waiting limousine. Wow, I thought, this was not bad. Driving through the city of London, which was, by the way, enormous, this gentleman pointed out all the sights just as any accomplished tour guide. It took me a while to fully understand him. He had a very proper English accent, and I think I finally got everything he said as we turned down the street where Linda and Tim lived.

That weekend I was shown every tourist attraction imaginable, including concerts at St. Martin's of the Field, museums, Buckingham palace, Prince Albert Hall, Kensington Palace and all the beautiful parks throughout London. However, it seemed that the most prominent sort of attraction came in the form of the "English Pub." The most noteworthy was the *Anglesea Arms*. We also took a memorable train ride into the country. The landscape was similar to the countryside of Germany and for that matter much of Europe which I would see on subsequent visits. We took the Eurostar under the English Channel to Paris. This took all of my courage as I didn't and still don't know how to swim. The young people, Linda and Tim, only laughed. It was great though and took only 20 minutes to get from England to the continent – as the Brits called it.

Paris is a story onto itself. The beautiful palaces and architecture – arches, bridges and statues, the Champs-Élysées. I couldn't pronounce many of the names and had to rely on the young people for spelling and pronunciation. It was amazing and beautiful. The cafés and neighborhoods along narrow alleys and watching the people go by was one of my favorite memories. It was a good decision to wear sensible low heeled shoes as all the streets appeared to be cobblestone. I always wondered why we in the States never used cobblestones. Maybe then we wouldn't have to fix those nasty pot holes every year that erupt in our pavements – all those summer detours just making traffic worse. Then again, the Parisian's don't have the number of roads or people driving on them as we do? Ah well, food for thought. Speaking of food…. Well, that will come later.

Another year, while Linda and Tim were living abroad, Linda and I went to Rome. This was one of the best art and history lessons I ever had with all of these ancient buildings and ruins. The Vatican with its square and all the other grand plazas, fountains, castles and monuments gave me such a powerful memory.

I had reservations whenever my children spoke of travelling somewhere new. They always wanted to schlep me along, and I always said no at first, but eventually I agreed to go and never regretted any one of those "forced" trips. One year it was Salzburg and I could almost see Julie Andrews marching by with her flock of Van Trapps! St. Stephan in Vienna was another visit – awesome. My cousins Annie and Maria who grew up outside Vienna, took us up to the top of St. Stephan's to the observation tower in order that we might see the beautiful colored roof tiles more closely. Walking through the cathedral's nave you could almost hear the Vienna Choir Boys if you closed your eyes. Someday I think I'd like to trace our journey from Rumania through the Danube River through Budapest and then Prague, through Germany and then finally coming through New York... before I get too old.

Back in the states, I was greeted with another grandchild. What a brave girl, my Maria was. You could say she drove herself to the hospital for the delivery. She was going initially for a check-up but she was clearly ready to deliver and so they kept her. Finally a boy for the Olsons! Rick and Maria named him Lukas and of course, his two sisters were not the only ones feeling *überglücklich*. We all were.

His first word was "car." As he got older, he would take a nap on my bed on my days off. When he awoke, he would rattle off the names of my children who were pictured in photos above my head board. He would start, "Tante Patti, Tante Linda, my mom, Onkel Richie and Lukas" he would say, even though the picture was of my son, Alex. He would argue with me when I tried to tell him it was not him. It's a marvelous thing, a little child's mind and seeing how the little wheels begin to work on new words and ideas. It's a shame they grow up so fast.

I mentioned our last family trip was to Colorado, but prior to that we took our fair share of vacations with the family – usually by car. Canada was a favorite destination. Richard had family there. His cousin Margret was married to a French Canadian, Gerald Rivest, whom she met while both were working for their respective embassies in Washington, D.C. back in the 1950's. They have three children, François, André and Véronique and while our children were growing up we saw each other frequently, driving between Ottawa, Canada and Chicago, Illinois, alternating sites. This was long before seat belt wearing became the law, and we made it safely each and every time. It was during one of those trips a long time ago when the Canadians visited us, that one day Gerald drove the children to the beach in Evanston. Upon their return, they entered the house laughing uncontrollably. Gerald explained in his heavily-accented English, that as he was driving down one of the streets all of a sudden a then four-year-old Richie yelled to him, "You're driving down the wrong side of the street, dummy!" Apparently he had been driving the wrong way on one of the many one-way streets when my son became alarmed and screamed this out at him. We never let him forget about that! Coming from a four-year old. This little memory continues to bring a laugh every time we retell it.

When Lukas was seven, the family took a vacation to again see our cousins in Ottawa, Canada. The Olson's went in one car, Patti, Linda and I drove in another car and Tim and Richie flew in as they were short on time. Gerald and Margret had invited us to their golden anniversary and Margret's 80th birthday. This was a huge fest. We stayed at the Westin Hotel a bit down the street from Parliament. You could see a corner of it from our room. The Rivests lived just across the Rideau River in Gatineau. You could see their apartment building from the bridge just this side of the river. We decided to walk across the bridge to see them. It seemed a lot closer than it really was but this turned out to be fortunate for us as it allowed us enough exercise to try to counterbalance all the food we were to intake the very next day.

After the church service marking their anniversary we drove in a caravan through Gatineau Park to a truly storybook-like house in the middle of the forest. Flanked by a large kitchen garden, a big white tent welcomed all the guests. A private path through the forest provided a quiet sanctuary for their guests and the children took full advantage. Dinner was served in this huge tent that opened up to a grand garden which included a swing. What genius – this way the adults could keep an eye on the children as they sipped champagne and mingled among the guests.

Many came from far away and had not seen each other for a long, long time and so the *Wiedersehen* included much hugging, laughing and singing. François, his wife Luz and their children Mariko and Louis Phillipe had come all the way from China. Their son André with Julie and his son Adrian came from Montreal. Véronique with husband Dominique and sons Theo and Felix were the only ones who lived nearby – just a few minutes' drive from this park. Their home is situated on a lake and when you come down to the pier, it almost appears as if the whole lake belongs to them for the houses around are nestled so far into the woods, you just see forest and green around the edges – very tranquil. I am quite certain her parents are happy to have them so nearby.

My children and grandchildren loved the lake. All of them, old and young, were in and out of the lake all weekend long. We had several picnics on the large deck off the kitchen with everyone pitching in to cook. It was a wonderful reunion for all of us as we hadn't been able to see each other with the same frequency as we had in the past. Can't wait for the next one! We talked about this trip endlessly when we returned to Chicago. Actually, I don't live in Chicago, but rather in Skokie, a suburb that when you think about it, is really an extension of that great windy city.

On the topic of Golden anniversaries, a few years earlier, our St. Alphonsus choir celebrated its 50th anniversary of singing beautiful music together. Fifty years with the same director, Herr Schoepko, who tirelessly put up with and developed a rambunctious group of kids into a dedicated church choir. Most of those celebrating fifty years had been with the choir from the very beginning – a loyalty not many choirs can boast. The pastor at the time of this anniversary, Father Hurlbert had been accommodating and gracious to this German choir as had all the preceding pastors at St. Alphonsus, in letting us continue to celebrate our mass in German. This anniversary was especially fine as our very own Francis Cardinal George, presided over the mass with Father Hurlbert. It was a special honor for us to be recognized in this manner. The *Chicago Tribune* even sent a reporter to cover the event and the next day there was a terrific write-up in the paper about us. The church has since gone through a complete restoration and is now easily one of the finest examples of gothic architecture in Chicago that should be seen by everyone.

As of this writing, our choir still can be heard singing here on Christmas and Easter and every first Sunday of the month. The German community comes from all over the Chicagoland area to celebrate these holidays with us in this magnificent church. The children and grandchildren of the choir members continue to return and celebrate the mass and the choir every year. It remains a strong and meaningful tradition for me and the rest of the 50-plus year members.

Chapter 11

It Takes More Than A Village

It was right around the time of that Golden Anniversary, that I was able to finally retire. It was something I couldn't at first comprehend but realized quickly I would be able to spend much more time with my grandchildren – what a gift! Another item on my retirement agenda was to travel more. At that particular time, both Patti and Linda were living outside of the Chicago area so this would provide ample opportunities to exercise my *wanderlust*.

I decided to embark on my travels immediately so after Christmas that first year, I flew with Patti down to Charlotte, North Carolina and then drove the rest of the way to her home in Columbia, South Carolina where she lived. My plans were to stay for the month of January and thereby miss all of that lovely winter weather up in Chicago. The very first thing I noticed on our trip was the absolute perfect condition of their roads, as though they had just been paved – must be the absence of all that winter snow and ice. No wonder BMW decided to build a plant down here. You can zoom down the roads with no bumps, cracks and potholes… and less traffic. The landscape was perfectly green and lush. Even in January, much of the Carolinas was still green with blooming bushes and even some flowers. Quite a contrast to the grey snowy scenes I had left behind.

I found the people were so pleasantly different there. They greeted you in passing – a perfect stranger greeted by another perfect stranger. The men held doors open for the women. Were we in the same country? Is it because we live in such a big city back home that people forget their proper manners? Is it because it's just so darn cold up there? They also dress very elegantly in the South. The men in button down shirt, tie and jacket almost everywhere we went – especially for church. While the women dressed refreshingly feminine, it was so nostalgic and yet also classy.

On the weekends, Patti would take me to various cities nearby. One time it was Charleston, another time it was Savannah. We also stayed in some beautiful B & B's in Asheville, Greenville, and Charlotte. Each city was distinctly scenic and bustling with tourists – especially Charleston & Savannah. We marveled at the beautiful old houses that had survived the Civil War. All that history, still evident made me appreciate how good and strong our country is despite how almost self- destructive we were.

Sometimes on my journeys down South, some of the kids would accompany me. Kiawah Island was a favorite spot. We headed there once with Linda, Tim, my son Rich and my nephew, Mike who lived in nearby Atlanta. The setting was beautiful – but the ocean was awesome, almost scary to me. The kids would head down to the beach at night for a nightcap. I passed on that invitation. The image of alligators slithering around in the swamps just itching to get a nibble of my ankles was enough to keep me safely indoors. Yuck!

Linda and I made our last trip down South by car to help move Patti back up to Chicago in 2009. What a trip that turned out to be. The two of us driving, well actually Linda did all of the driving, through rain storm after rain storm even on through the Blue Ridge mountains. It reminded me of driving through the Black forest – powerful and majestic. My knuckles were tight and white as Linda made each twist and turn of that mountain pass through the sheeting rain. Boy, were we glad to finally reach Columbia. Rich had flown down to help us – he was the smart one. We spent that vacation mostly working, packing boxes and cleaning up the house and after a lovely garden party hosted by one of Patti's friends, we said our goodbye's headed back for home.

One year, Linda, Patti, Tim and I flew out to Germany to visit with relatives we hadn't seen in a long time and for me to show them some of the sites where I had grown. Patti and I flew separately and after landing in Frankfurt immediately set out for Heidelberg. We were to meet Linda and Tim there who had rented a car for the trip. Boy did that come in handy. We traveled almost the entire *Romantische Strasse*! Staying in small hotels on the Bodensee and Rothenburg taking in all the beautiful sights and flavors! It was delicious. I showed them Wettringen, the small village where I had grown up with its river, der Tauber. It seemed so much smaller from what I remembered. I introduced them to my dear friend, Traudl and the two of us walked arm-in-arm through the streets of Rothenburg, just as we had over 50 years ago!

Our trip also included a rendezvous with the Canadians – Margret and Gerald – in Osnabruck. We reunited with Fraulein Witte, a close friend of the Sudendorf family for a wonderful dinner in this post-war city and then made our way to Alfhausen and Neuenkirchen to visit with some of Richard's relatives, some of whom I'd not seen in years and years. Once we were sitting in their *guten Stube*, however, we all caught up with each other's news and fell into familiar conversation with the accompanying *Schnapps* and *Kaffee*!

Back in Chicago again, everyone was back to work except for me and I couldn't wait to spend more time with the grandchildren and tell them stories of all of our adventures. My son-in-law Rick had a job that took him away from home during the week so I gladly helped out Maria as much as I could with all the kids' goings-on. The kids would always ask me to cook them something, mostly requesting either *Pfannenkuchen* or *Schmarren* and I would gladly oblige.

Aside from what seemed like mountains and mountains of homework, Olivia and Julia spent a lot of time playing soccer and volleyball or cross country, while Lukas was involved in speed skating, hockey and whatever other sport Rick had signed him up for. There was always a need for an extra driver and I was happy to volunteer, despite my fear...rather hatred of driving. The kids were just so sweet. Whenever I drove Lukas anywhere, he always asked if I could spend the night in the "neighbor's bed." I stayed whenever I could and we would tell stories way into the night.

Surprise! More good news came late in 2009. After years of trying, finally, Tim and Linda were expecting a baby. What a joy! The long anticipated event was just at our doorsteps. A sweet, little girl, Mia Kimberly was born in May of 2010 and is our newest little angel. The whole family hovers over her. Our family and Tim's family are all just so taken by this little baby. Just like my Mia's kids, I quickly volunteered to take care of her whenever Linda needed. I love taking care of her – mostly at my condo – there are no stairs that I have to climb, it's much smaller and so I can follow her around a lot easier especially since she started walking – I mean running! Her first words were, "Go! Go!" – not "mommy" or "daddy." Imagine where this will be going?

Mia's first birthday was a big deal, as you might expect. Everyone was invited, as usual. But with such a large family you can expect a lot of celebrations. It was just a few months earlier that we had celebrated Luke's First Communion, then there was Olivia's confirmation and then graduation, Julia's plays, you name it. There's always so much laughter and good food. It's almost impossible to lose just a few pounds – there's never a normal week. Along with my sister and brothers' family events, we're always raising a glass and a fork to something or other.

Speaking of family events, I would be seriously remiss if I didn't write about our annual family Christmas celebrations. Since the time both my parents were still alive, my sister, Pat, my brothers, Adi, Tony and Al, and our families would come together every Christmas Eve to enjoy the holiday with each other. When my mom was still alive she would always host this fest with delicious and plentiful homemade treats that she prepared especially for this holiday. After her passing, the surviving children made a pact to continue this tradition and rotate the responsibility of hosting the entire family among the five of us. This brought on a good amount of healthy and maybe not-so-healthy competition for who could provide the most lavish banquet and who could stay most "true" to Oma's cooking. We continue this tradition to this day with their children and their children's children totaling over 40 strong. Try accommodating that group in a two-bedroom condo!

The children delight us with caroling and the much anticipated re-enactment of the Christmas nativity. Each of the grandchildren plays a role and with the recent spate of newborn babies, we've been able to have a "real" baby Jesus dressed in swaddling clothes! And what Christmas Eve gathering would be complete without our rendition of "The Twelve Days of Christmas?"

Sometimes, though, we have to get together not to celebrate but rather to mourn. Lately, I've been going to more wakes and funerals of cousins, second and third cousins or their parents and when I run into this extended family we complain about not making the time to see each other under happier circumstances.

Then, just a few months ago, one of my many cousins had their golden anniversary and decided to invite all of the extended family to their celebration. Tina, my second cousin and her husband, Walter Ronge hosted this lovely celebration. Tina's mother is a cousin to my mother and Tina's father was a cousin to my father. So you can see how closely connected we really are! There were some 100 cousins there and that's not counting the next generation of children and grandchildren. I roughly counted the extended family and got to about 231 that all lived in the Chicago area. Unbelievable, isn't it? It was so touching seeing all the familiar faces – maybe somewhat older, but not less beautiful and *herzlich*. I just can't find the right English word to convey this feeling.

Thanks to my son, Rich, we have resurrected an old tradition of yearly picnics of this extended family in Harms Woods. When we first came to this country, my family and our extended family would meet one Saturday afternoon in the summer for the kids to run around, the men to argue and play cards and the women to catch up on all the latest happenings and compare whose *Kartoffelsalat* was better. It was a great opportunity for the kids to get to know one another and for the grown-ups to stay in touch even though everyone was moving further and further from Chicago.

Rich would oftentimes ask me, "Exactly how are we related to so-and-so?" after seeing a cousin of mine downtown or at a soccer function. Even I would oftentimes have to take out the old family tree book to look it up, although I pride myself at knowing most of the family connections. There are just so many of us. I think it was these musings that finally prompted Rich to take charge and get this tradition back on track so that he would have a better understanding and relationship with this large extended family.

Every spring Rich would send out an email asking for good dates for the family picnic and then get the required permit. On the day selected for that year everyone would come to the reserved site at the forest preserve with their baskets full of homemade salads, cakes, breads and you name it. We would provide the grills and made certain we got our bratwursts from Paulina Market. It just wasn't a proper picnic without brats from Paulina. Some years back Rich even had some large banners made advertising the cousins' picnic which he sets up early in the morning with a few select volunteers.

As the others arrive, they all laid claim to one of the many picnic tables gathered in our favorite spot. Each family then begins to empty out their goodies and they are laid out to be shared by everyone. Onkel Florian, my mom's youngest brother, his wife, Tante Hilde and my Tante Monica would come just as they had so many years ago when we first came to this country, to that very first picnic and would hold court. As everyone settles in the kids start to run around, the men argue and play cards and the women catch up on the current happenings while watching the little ones out of the corners of their eyes. In the background you can hear fiery and romantic German tunes coming from our own disc jockey – Karl Bauer. A perfect summer day! Back home our parents used to say "*Wie im Wäldche,*" or "Just like in the woods."

I so look forward to it every year. Watching the young ones meet one another while we, the older generation sit back brimming with pride over this younger generation. They've inherited so much from their parents' diligence and hard labor. They are now the established ones – excelling in the careers they've chosen as teachers, doctors, dentists, attorneys, businesspeople, shop owners, financiers, coaches, soccer players, engineers, soldiers, farmers and citizens, they are the real Americans.

* * *

As has been said, "It takes a village." I would add, for an immigrant, it takes a generation of family to raise a true American. Our children are the proof. Our country can only be richer for all of the immigrant families that have influenced their children and their children's children. It was the back-breaking work and perseverance of my parents, my grandparents, my cousins and brothers and sister that made this reluctant immigrant finally find home for herself and her family.

Alois Mueller, paternal grandfather circa 1930.

Mathias Mueller, my father harvesting in Rumania, circa 1930–32

Inhabitants of the *Lager*, in Austria – half of them were our relatives! Circa 1941

My sister, Perpetua, brother Adi and I in Bischkowitz, Czechoslovakia, circa 1943

Returning from church, Onkel Clemens and cousin Mathias in driver's seat, circa 1944

Our family in Wettringen, Germany, surrounding my grandmother, circa 1949

Our living quarters in Wettringen, Germany – we lived on the first floor,
circa 1949

Our arrival in the U.S. on
the hottest day in July, 1955

The St. Alphonsus German Choir, Chicago IL, circa 1956

Tante Anna and Onkel Ben
Suden, Dick's Aunt and
Uncle, May 1953

Dick Sudendorf returned from Korea, 1956

Dick and I attending a wedding before we were married, 1957

Our wedding, photo of bride and family, 1957

Rich's Chicago Kicker's soccer team – he's in the top middle
with arms crossed, 1978

Girl's All-Star soccer team, Patti is 5th from the left, top row,
and Linda is front row left lying on the grass – the goalie, 1977

Our family's trip to Vail, Colorado, 1977

The kids at Christmas, 1986

Making cookie houses for St. Lambert's, 1984

Cookie house
of St. Paschal in
Chicago, 1984

St. Lambert's Choir, 2008

My siblings and I on our reunion trip to Rothenburg ob der Taube,
Germany, 1996

Ehmann's Traudel and I walking through the streets of Rothenburg
with Linda and Patti, 2008

The grandchildren caroling with some of their cousins, singing Stille Nacht, 2005

Rick and Maria Olson's crew at the Christkindlemarkt, Chicago;
Julia, Olivia & Lucas, 2004

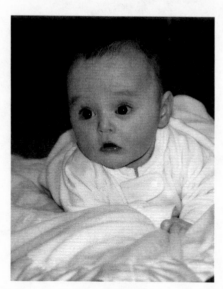

Tim and Linda Ransford's,
"baby" Mia, 2010

Onkel Florian's 80th Birthday celebration, 2004

From Margret and Gerald Rivest's wedding invitation,
(Married 1959 – anniversary 2009)

Tina and Walter Ronge's Golden Wedding Anniversary cake, 2010

Family picture, 2011

Felizitas Sudendorf

Intro to Recipes

As with any immigrant experience, the richness of one's heritage flows from food. Ours was no different. Throughout this book you therefore found many references to food and especially, the home cooked meals my mother and her generation prepared for us regularly. I was lucky enough to have learned from my mother how to prepare some of these meals from recipes that have been passed down from generation to generation. I needed to translate them to something that would be more easily identifiable to my kids and anyone else who would like to try a hand at them. I would often be

Cousin Kenny and Patti inspecting one of our many Easter spreads, circa 1990

asked: How much is a *Schuck* exactly? What does *geschmältzte* mean? How many different varieties of *Mehlspeis* are there? Do they all "knead" yeast? How does that work? I also included a few recipes that we love from friends and relatives and have given them the recognition they well deserve for sharing these special delicacies.

So for my kids and my American compatriots – here goes....

Ze Menu

Appetizers

Linda's artichoke dip

Liptauer Käse – *Liptauer cheese*

Schinkensalat – *ham salad*

Herringsalat – *herring salad*

Tante Margret's tapenade

Oma's Mehlspeis – flour-based dishes

Küchle – *fried dough*

Geschmälzte Knödel – *gnocchi sautéed in onions*

Käsblätz – *cheese pockets*

Pierogi

Dampfnudel – *dumplings*

Kaiser Schmarren – *scrambled pancakes with raisins & nuts*

Pfannkuchen – *crepes/sweet or savory*

Ze Menu

Main Courses

Schnitzel – *veal & pork cutlets*

Chicken Schnitzlets

Kassler mit Süssem Kraut – *roast pork with sweet slaw*

Kartoffel im Röhr – *roast chicken with potatoes*

Huhn im rice – *chicken and rice*

Reh Goulash mit Nudeln – *venison goulash with noodles*

Hungarian Goulash

Gefüllte Pfeffern – *stuffed peppers*

Krautwickel – *stuffed cabbage*

Gyulai sausage und Kraut – *sausage and warm slaw*

Konigsberger Klops – *meatballs bohemian style*

Rouladen – *beef rolls*

Ze Menu

Vegetables, Soups & Salads

Rösti Potatoes – *roasted potatoes*

Kartoffelpfannkuchen – *potato pancakes, sweet or savory*

Weiser Spargel mit Kreme Sosse –
white asparagus with cream sauce

Blumenkohlsalat – *cauliflower salad*

Rosenkohlsalat – *Brussels sprout salad*

Rote Beete Salat – *red beet salad*

Möhrensalat – *carrot and celery root salad*

Gurkensalat – *cucumber salad*

Kartoffelsalat – *potato salad*

Linsen Suppe – *lentil soup*

Ze Menu

Desserts

Leni's Apfelschnitten – *apple slices*

Oma's Zwetschgenkuchen – *plum cake*

Oma's Streuselkuchen – *streusel coffee cake*

Tante Margret's Apfelmusskuchen – *apple sauce cake*

Obst Kompott – *fruit compote*

Frau Schoepko's Rice Pudding with Apricots

Liz's Taffy Apple Salad

Obst Torte – *seasonal fruit tart*

Mr. McKay's Cheesecake

Opa Sudendorf's Cream Puffs

Ze Menu

Seasonal Dishes

Betty Bachmeier's Christstollen

Margret Traub's Juliana Schnitten – *nut squares*

Spritzgebäck – *butter cookies*

Patti's Carmelitas

Margret Traub's Fasching's Krapfen – *Lenten bismarks*

Leni's Mom's Hörnchen – *crescent rolls*

Oster Stritzel – *Easter braided bread*

APPETIZERS

LINDA'S ARTICHOKE DIP

2 cans artichoke hearts (chopped)
2 cups grated Parmesan cheese
2 cups mayonnaise
1 package Good Seasons garlic & herb salad dressing mix

Mix all ingredients together; pour into shallow baking dish
and bake at 350° F until top is bubbly and beginning to brown.
Serve warm with crackers or crusty bread.

LIPTAUER KÄSE– Liptauer Cheese

1 stick butter, room temperature
½ lb. farmer's cheese or goat cheese (room temperature)
1 onion, finely diced
3 anchovy fillets, finely chopped
1 tablespoon caraway seeds
½ teaspoon paprika

Place butter in blender and blend until creamy, slowly add the cheese incorporating into butter, then add onions and anchovies. Finely blend in the caraway seeds and the paprika. The final *Käse* should have the consistency of cream cheese. You can serve immediately with crackers or pumpernickel or refrigerate. Can last up to a week refrigerated.

SCHINKENSALAT – ham salad

1 lb. thickly sliced boiled ham
½ lb. Emmental cheese
4 medium sized dill pickles
2 granny smith apples, peeled and cored
½ onion, finely diced
½ cup mayonnaise
½ cup sour cream
Salt & pepper

Slice the ham into one-inch strips and then julienne the strips (easiest by stacking the one-inch strips). Do the same with the cheese, pickles and the apples. Combine in bowl, and add finely diced onion. Mix together sour cream and mayonnaise and add to ingredients. Salt & pepper to taste. Serve immediately with crackers, dark rye is especially tasty – as appetizer or also as a sandwich. Salad can be refrigerated for up to a week.

HERRINGSALAT – herring salad

¾ lb herring fillet
½ lb. boiled veal
3 medium potatoes, boiled and peeled
3 medium red beets, boiled and peeled
3 granny smith apples
1 red onion
1 tablespoon capers
Salt & pepper
Splash white wine vinegar
½ cup red wine, dry
½ cup sour cream
½ cup mayonnaise

Cut herring, veal, potatoes, beets, apples and onion into small pieces and combine in bowl. Add capers then salt & pepper to taste. Add splash of white wine vinegar and pour red wine over ingredients. Mix and refrigerate covered overnight. The next day add the sour cream. Ready to serve. Can be served as an appetizer but also as a dinner with boiled potatoes and your favorite vegetable.

TANTE MARGRET RIVEST'S TAPENADE

1 ½ cup crushed Kalamata olives
3 anchovy fillets, finely diced
1 tablespoon capers, finely diced
3 garlic cloves, finely diced
Juice of ½ lemon

Mix together finely diced olives, anchovy, capers and garlic.
Pour in lemon juice. Combine completely. Serve on toasted
crostini or with French baguette (*mais bien sur!*)

KÜCHLE – fried dough

2 cups warm water
5 cups pre-sifted flour
2 packages yeast
1 tablespoon sugar
3 eggs, room temperature
2 cups frying oil, or Crisco (or *Schmaltz* (lard), if you can find any – Oma always used this!)

SERVES 8

Heat water to 110° F. In a mixing bowl put in flour and make a dent in the middle where you sprinkle in the yeast then the sugar. Pour ½ cup of the heated water slowly into the dent and stir slowly making a paste in the middle. Do not use all of the flour, just the paste in the middle. Sprinkle some flour over the top. Let it sit aside in a warm spot until you see cracks forming on top of your "yeast volcano." In the meantime, beat the eggs.

Combine eggs and the remaining water with "yeast volcano" and knead the ingredients together with your hands until all of the dough comes cleanly off your hands. If it sticks, add some more flour. Take the dough out and put a splash of vegetable oil in the bowl and then roll the dough around the bowl until your dough is shiny.

Cover dough in bowl with lint-free dishtowel and then put another bath towel over it and place in the warmest spot in your house. Please keep away from any drafts, vents, air conditioners, etc. Let the dough rise – should take approximately one hour.

Once dough has risen, prepare a large cutting board by sprinkling a little flour and spreading around. Form dough into a long roll about the size of a French baguette. Cut into two-inch pieces. Roll each piece into a ball, flouring your hands every so often so the dough doesn't stick. Do this with each piece and place back on cutting board, ensuring the pieces do not touch each other. Cover the balls with lint-free dish towel and let rise in warm corner, preferably near the stove.

In the meantime pour the oil (Crisco or *Schmaltz*) into a 1½ quart pot. Heat the oil until you see ringlets forming at the bottom of the pot. Take one of the balls and dip one edge into the oil and then stretch the dough out in your hands. Your hands should also be oily. Then slowly stretch the dough so that it's about the size of the rim of the quart pot. The edges of the dough should be thicker than the middle. Place gently into oil and let it sit until the edges of the bottom become golden brown. Turn the dough over using tongs and let the other side cook until golden brown. Remove and let cool. They can be stacked on top of each other like pancakes. Repeat with each roll. Salt lightly. Best when served immediately and with a hearty soup like navy bean or split pea (recipes to follow). You can also eat them cold.

GESCHMÄLZTE KNÖDEL – gnocchi sautéed in onions

4 ½ cups flour
1 tablespoon salt
1 egg
2 cups water – room temperature
4 strips bacon, diced
2 yellow onions, coarsely diced
2 tablespoons vegetable oil (or bacon fat, if you're really
feeling indulgent)

SERVES 8

In a bowl pour the flour and salt and make a dent in the middle
with your fist. Crack an egg into the dent, cover with a thin film
of flour and pour some of the warm water slowly around the
edges of the flour. Begin kneading dough with your hands and
continue to add water until dough comes easily off your hands.
Form a loose ball and set aside. Let it sit for about 30 minutes.

Prepare your cutting board by spreading flour on the board
and roll your dough into a long roll about the size of a French
baguette. Cut roll into one-inch pieces. Take each piece and
stretch it into a long thin pencil-like shape. Flatten it into 2-inch
strips and cut into matchstick size pieces. Remove to a floured
cookie sheet – pieces should be separate and shouldn't touch. Let
dry. Repeat with each one-inch piece.

Get out your pasta pot and fill ¾ full with water. Add salt and a
drop of olive oil. Bring pot to boil. Using a spatula, put all the
gnocchi's into the pot making sure they're not sticking to each
other. Keep water at a boil and cook until all of the gnocchi have

risen to the top. Take one out and test it to make sure it's cooked throughout. It should be a similar consistency to al dente pasta. Drain gnocchi and put aside.

In a large skillet, sauté diced bacon and onions in vegetable oil until onions are translucent. Turn off the heat, then add gnocchi and stir until all of the gnocchi are covered with bacon/onion sauce. Can be served on its own, as a pasta – we like it with goulash!

KÄSBLÄTZ – cheese pockets

4 ½ cups flour
1 tablespoon salt
1 egg
2 cups water (or milk) – room temperature

For filling:
1 lb farmer's cheese
½ lb boiled ham, finely chopped pieces
1 egg
½ cup sour cream

SERVES 8

In a bowl pour the flour and salt and make a dent in the middle
with your fist. Crack an egg into the dent, cover with a thin film
of flour and pour some of the warm water slowly around the
edges of the flour. Begin kneading dough with your hands and
continue to add water until dough comes easily off your hands.
Form a loose ball and set aside. Let it sit for about 30 minutes.

In the meantime, mix farmer's cheese, finely chopped ham,
1 egg, sour cream together in a bowl.

When your dough has rested, shape the dough into a long roll
about the size of a French baguette. Cut this roll into ½-inch
pieces. Roll each ½-inch piece with a rolling pin making a thin
oval about the size of a large hand. Place a spoonful of your
filling in the middle and then flip it over so that it forms a
half-moon. Pinch together the sides to make certain filling is
tightly sealed in the dough. If it's not sticking, put a little water

at the end which will help to seal the dough. Repeat with
each piece.

In a large quart pot, add 3 cups vegetable oil (you can also use
Schmalz or Crisco – makes them more crispy). Heat the oil until
you can see small ringlets on the bottom of the pot. Put two
Käsblätz in at a time. Fry until golden brown then turn them
around careful not to pierce the dough. Once both sides are
brown, remove with a pasta strainer and set aside. Repeat with
each *Käsblätz*. Serve immediately – best when nice and warm
with a cup of bouillon!

PIEROGI

4 ½ cups flour
1 tablespoon salt
1 egg
2 cups water – room temperature

For filling:
8 oz farmer's cheese
4 oz cream cheese
1 egg
Chives or dill to taste

For topping:
2–3 slices bacon
1 cup breadcrumbs
2 tablespoon butter

SERVES 8

In a bowl pour the flour and salt and make a dent in the middle with your fist. Crack an egg into the dent, cover with a thin film of flour and pour some of the warm water slowly around the edges of the flour. Begin kneading dough with your hands and continue to add water until dough comes easily off your hands. Form a loose ball and set aside. Let it sit for about 30 minutes.

In a separate bowl combine the farmer's cheese, cream cheese, egg and chives or dill. Set aside.

Prepare your cutting board by spreading a thin layer of flour across it. Remove the dough ball and place it in the middle of your surface and then flatten using the balls of your hands. Flour your rolling pin and then begin rolling out your dough as thin as you can without tearing it. You may need to flip your dough several times during this process – this will help you gauge the firmness you will need for folding the dough.

Using either a pasta cutter, cookie cutter or even a knife, cut the dough into rounds or squares. In the middle of each place a spoonful of the cheese mixture. Then fold over the sides of the dough and pinch together to seal the cheese mixture inside. The finished product should look like either a triangle or half moon, depending on what kind of cutter you're using. Place the sealed pierogi on a floured, lint-free dish towel and line them up until you've finished forming each one.

Fill a large pasta cooking pot three-quarters full with water and add a teaspoon of salt and a drop of olive oil. Bring this to a boil. Drop in your pierogi one by one and cook uncovered, stirring frequently. When the pierogi have the texture of al dente pasta – they're finished.

For topping, fry bacon in skillet and crumble. Add breadcrumbs and stir until well coated. Pour over pierogi and serve.

DAMPFNUDEL – dumplings

2 cups warm milk
5 cups pre-sifted flour
2 packages yeast
1 tablespoon sugar
3 eggs, room temperature
¼ cup vegetable oil
2 pinches of salt
1 ½ cups water

SERVES 8

Heat milk to 110° F. In a mixing bowl put in flour and make
a dent in the middle where you sprinkle in the yeast then the
sugar. Pour ½ cup of the heated milk slowly into the dent and stir
slowly making a paste in the middle. Do not use all of the flour,
just the paste in the middle. Sprinkle some flour over the top.
Let it sit aside in a warm spot until you see cracks forming on
top of your "yeast volcano." In the meantime, beat the eggs.

Combine eggs and the remaining milk with "yeast volcano"
and knead the ingredients together with your hands until all of
the dough comes cleanly off your hands. If it sticks, add some
more flour. Take the dough out and put a splash of vegetable oil
in the bowl and then roll the dough around the bowl until your
dough is shiny.

Cover dough in bowl with lint-free dishtowel and then put
another bath towel over it and place in the warmest spot in your
house. Please keep away from any drafts, vents, air conditioners,
etc. Let the dough rise – should take approximately one hour.

Once dough has risen, prepare a large cutting board by sprinkling a little flour and spreading around. Form dough into a long roll about the size of a French baguette. Cut into two-inch pieces. Roll each piece into a ball, flouring your hands every so often so the dough doesn't stick. Do this with each piece and place back on cutting board ensuring the pieces do not touch each other. Cover the balls with lint-free dish towel and let rise in warm corner, preferably near the stove.

In a Dutch oven or deep frying pan, heat vegetable oil, sprinkle in 2 pinches of salt then add the water. When it starts to sputter, place the dumplings into the pan/oven touching each other, close together in a circular pattern. Cover with lid (best with Pyrex glass lid so that you can look at the dumplings without removing lid – they will collapse). Put flame to medium heat for about 30 minutes. Lift the pan on one side to hear if water is still sputtering. Once you no longer hear the water, immediately take off flame and let stand to the side with the lid closed for 15–20 minutes.

After 20 minutes, take off the lid and with a spatula remove the dumplings from the pan. The bottoms of the dumplings should have a nice golden brown crust to them. Serve with chicken fricassee, beef bourguignon or Sloppy Joe's.

KAISER SCHMARREN – scrambled pancakes

3 eggs
3 cups flour
3 cups milk
1 cup vegetable or canola oil

For Kaiser's topping:
1 stick butter
1 cup raisins
1 cup sugar
1 cup chopped nuts (optional)
¼ cup milk

SERVES 6

In a medium/large mixing bowl, beat the eggs. Then add 2
tablespoons flour and 2 tablespoons milk; stir until clumps disap-
pear. Repeat process, adding flour, then milk, until batter is the
consistency of pancake batter (or pudding). Cover bowl and let
mixture "rest" for about 1 hour, stirring occasionally.

In a deep frying pan, heat vegetable oil until water sizzles when
spritzed upon the surface. Add *Schmarren* mixture to pan and
let brown on sides and bottom. Cover for 3 minutes. Then begin
to turn as you would scrambled eggs, so that mixture slowly
browns on all sides and forms bite-sized pieces. This is easiest
when using two forks to separate. Transfer to serving bowl.

Meanwhile, in a small saucepan, melt butter. Then add raisins,
sugar, nuts and milk, gently warming mixture until sugar is

dissolved. When *Schmarren* are ready, pour sauce over the top and serve immediately. We usually serve it with warm compote.

PFANNKUCHEN – crepes

6 eggs
Pinch of salt
1 tablespoon vegetable oil
1 tablespoon water
3 cups flour
3 cups milk

MAKES 20 PFANNENKUCHEN*

Whisk together eggs, salt, vegetable oil and water until everything is well integrated. Add 2 tablespoons of flour and ½ cup
milk and whisk until smooth – no lumps. Repeat this procedure
until all of the flour and milk are fully incorporated. The batter
should be the consistency of gravy – not as stiff as traditional
pancake patter. Set aside uncovered for one hour.

After an hour, whisk once through and then heat a small amount
of oil or Crisco in a frying pan. When the oil is hot, pour a ladle
of batter into the pan and swirl around the pan until the batter
completely coats the bottom of the pan. This should fry on
medium heat. When the edges become golden brown, flip it over.
Remove the crepe by folding it over and transporting it to a platter. Repeat until all the batter is gone. Fill the crepe with your
favorite sweets or savories! On special occasions, we like sliced
smoked ham and white asparagus in cream sauce.

*For a variation, add peeled and sliced apples to batter and fry
for *Apfelpfannkuchen*!

1

MAIN COURSES

SCHNITZEL MIT ROTEM KRAUT – veal or pork cutlets with red cabbage

1 cup flour
2 eggs, beaten
2 tablespoons milk or water
1 cup breadcrumbs
6 veal or pork boneless cutlets, (should be no thicker than ½-inch)
Salt & pepper
1 ¼ cup vegetable oil
Small head red cabbage
1 large yellow onion
Juice of half a lemon
Salt & pepper to taste
1 peeled apple

SERVES 6

Prepare 3 shallow bowls – put flour in one, put beaten eggs and water/milk in another, and the third fill with bread crumbs (you can also crush zwieback or saltines with a rolling pin if you don't have bread crumbs). First beat the meat thin, then salt & pepper cutlets on both sides. Then one at a time, using a fork, dip cutlet into flour and press firmly on both sides, then dip into egg mixture, then dip into bread crumbs and press firmly to make sure crumbs stay on cutlet. Set aside and repeat process with each cutlet. Let them set at room temperature for 10–15 minutes.

Put 1 cup vegetable oil in frying pan and heat on high until when spritzed with a small droplet of water, the oil sputters. (Caution: stay far enough away so that you don't get the hot oil spritzed on YOU!) Lower flames to medium then put two cutlets in at a time, and fry on both sides until golden brown. Repeat process with remaining cutlets. Serve immediately with lemon wedges.

For cabbage, rinse head under cold water. Then cut off an inch from the stem. Towel dry and cut into 4 wedges. Slice each wedge into thin slaw. Cut onion into quarters and thinly slice onions in the same manner as cabbage. Heat remaining oil in deep frying pan until oil sizzles, add the onions and let simmer, add cabbage and then let it fry until the onions begin to brown. Keep stirring cabbage and onion so it doesn't stick to bottom of pan. About 15 minutes. Add lemon juice and grate in an apple. Salt & pepper to taste. Cover and continue to cook over low heat for 30 minutes, stirring occasionally.

Serve *Schnitzel* and cabbage with either mashed potatoes or German potato salad.

CHICKEN SCHNITZLETS

4 lbs. skinless chicken tenders
1 cup mayonnaise or yogurt
Salt & pepper
1 ½ cups bread crumbs
½ cup vegetable oil

SERVES 8

Rinse tenders and pat dry with paper towels. Place tenders in a large mixing bowl and add mayonnaise; stir to coat and season mixture generously with salt & pepper. Mix to blend, then cover and refrigerate for an hour, or overnight.

When ready to prepare, dip tenders individually into bread crumbs to give them a light coating. Once coated, allow chicken to rest for 10 minutes or so before cooking.

Heat oil in deep frying pan until it spritzes when a droplet of water hits it. Brown tenders – about 5 minutes per side or until cooked through. Drain on paper towels.

KASSLER MIT SÜSSEMKRAUT – smoked pork chops and sweet warm slaw

4 smoked pork chops (you can get these at Paulina Market or other fine butcher shops)
¼ cup vegetable oil
1 teaspoon coarse ground pepper
1 medium yellow onion
1 small head green cabbage
1 cube of chicken bouillon
3 tablespoons caraway seeds (you can add more or less, depending on taste)

SERVES 4

Rinse pork chops and then pat dry. In a deep frying pan, heat oil on medium heat. When oil is heated, sprinkle pork chops with course pepper and place in pan. Lightly brown both sides. Add sliced onions and let roast with the chops. Keep on medium heat.

In the meantime, core your green cabbage, cut in quarters and thinly shred. Place the cabbage over the meat and onions. Over the top, sprinkle one cube crumbled/powdered chicken bouillon. Pour in the caraway seeds. Cover and let cook for about 10 minutes. After 10 minutes stir so that pork chops are on top and the cabbage is on the bottom. Cover again and continue cooking for about 30 minutes. Turn it again, so that pork chops are on bottom and cabbage is on top and cook on very low flame for another 10–15 minutes. Serve with dark rye bread or mashed or *rösti* potatoes.

KARTOFFELN IM ROHR – chicken & potatoes

1 whole chicken
Salt & pepper to taste
1 teaspoon herbs de Provence
1 teaspoon dried rosemary
2 medium yellow onions
3 cloves garlic
6 Yukon gold potatoes
1 cup water
¼ cup olive oil

SERVES 4

Rinse chicken and pat dry. Remove any gizzards from inside
chicken and set aside. Salt & pepper chicken inside and out;
then add dried herbs. Place chicken in Dutch oven on its back.
If desired, tie legs together with cooking string. Peel and rinse
potatoes. Cut into quarters and place in pan around chicken.
Slice onion and add to pan. Crush garlic and spread over
chicken. Sprinkle potatoes with salt & pepper. Pour water over
potatoes and drizzle both potatoes and chicken with olive oil.

Place pan into pre-heated 375° F oven and roast for 1–1½ hours
or until meat thermometer reads 180° F when inserted into thick-
est part of chicken. If chicken is not yet done but getting too
brown, cover with foil loosely while you continue to roast.

When chicken and potatoes are done, remove from oven. Allow
chicken to rest, covered with foil, 10–15 minutes before carving.

HUHN IM RICE – chicken & rice

1 whole chicken, in pieces – or just breasts – whatever you like
Salt & pepper to taste
¼ cup vegetable oil
1 cup short grain rice
1 chicken bouillon cube
1 ½ cups warm water or white wine

SERVES 4

Pat chicken pieces dry and salt & pepper lightly on all sides. In a medium skillet, brown chicken in oil on all sides over medium heat. Remove chicken from pan. Pour rice into pan with chicken juices and add chicken bouillon cube, crumbled. Stir gently while rice begins to cook. When rice is translucent, add water and continue stirring gently. Return chicken to pot, cover and cook over medium heat for 45 minutes – 1 hour, checking occasionally. When rice is al dente, turn heat off, open lid and place a cheese cloth or lint-free dishcloth over the top of the pan, then re-cover with lid and allow mixture to steam gently without heat. Salt & pepper to taste, and serve.

REH GOULASH MIT NUDELN – venison goulash with noodles

For marinade:
Handful whole peppercorns
1 small onion, sliced
2 cloves garlic, sliced
2 bay leaves
3 teaspoon "salada" or salad vinegar
3 teaspoon extra virgin olive oil (EVOO)
Salt & pepper

1 ½ lbs. venison loin
2 carrots
1 yellow onion
1 cup dry red wine – divided
4 tablespoons sour cream or crème fraiche
1 tablespoon corn starch or flour
1 16 oz. package egg noodles

SERVES 6

Mix together all marinade ingredients and pour over venison loin in shallow dish. Cover with plastic wrap and refrigerate for 2–4 hours or overnight (turning occasionally).

Cut meat into bite-sized cubes. Sear marinated loin in EVOO in a medium skillet over medium-high heat on all sides. Add 2 chopped carrots and 1 chopped onion, plus remaining marinade, into pan. Cook over medium heat for 30 minutes, then add ½ cup red wine mixed with ½ cup warm water and add to pan. Cook another 30 minutes, or until liquid is reduced by half. Add another ½ cup red wine mixed with ½ cup warm water to pan. Cover and simmer over medium-low heat until meat is tender.

When meat is done, remove from pan. In a small bowl, whisk together sour (or sweet) cream with corn starch and add warm water slowly to make 1 cup of mixture in total. Aim for creamy consistency with no lumps. Pour into pan over low heat slowly, stirring to mix with pan juices to form gravy. Then add meat back into pan and keep warm.

Meanwhile, cook noodles in water until al dente. Drain and serve with goulash.

HUNGARIAN GOULASH

2 lbs. pork tenderloin

¼ cup vegetable oil

1 large white onion

2 carrots

3–4 sprigs fresh parsley (or 1 teaspoon dried)

Salt & pepper to taste

3 cloves garlic – chopped

2 bay leaves

1 chicken bouillon cube

2 tablespoons sweet paprika

½ cup sour cream

1 tablespoon flour

¼-ish cup of dry red wine (a *Schuck*)

1 teaspoon red pepper flakes (optional)

SERVES 6

Refrigerate tenderloin for 1 hour to firm up meat; then slice into rounds. Cut rounds into quarters. In a medium skillet, brown meat gently on all sides in vegetable oil. Meanwhile, dice onion and carrots; then add to skillet. Add garlic and bay leaves. Chop fresh parsley and add to skillet. Cover and cook briefly over medium heat. Salt & pepper to taste; then add 2 cups warm water and bouillon cube, along with paprika. Simmer for 30–45 minutes or until meat is tender. In a small bowl, mix sour cream with flour and a *Schuck* of wine and add to skillet, stirring gently. If desired, season with crushed ground red pepper flakes. Simmer for another 15 minutes. Serve with *Spätzle*, polenta or a nice flat butter noodle.

GEFÜLLTE PFEFFERN – stuffed peppers

4 green peppers
1 lb. ground pork or veal
½ cup uncooked short grain rice
1 egg
Salt & pepper
Red pepper flakes
2 cloves garlic – minced
¼ cup vegetable oil
3–4 new potatoes – peeled & sliced into quarters
2 stalks celery – chopped
1 small onion – chopped
1 cube chicken bouillon
1 28 oz. can diced tomatoes
¼ cup grated parmesan cheese

SERVES 6

Halve peppers, removing stems and interiors and rinse
thoroughly. Mix together the ground meat, rice, egg, salt, pepper,
red pepper and garlic. Fill each of the pepper halves with a
handful of the meat mixture (fill just to top).

Heat oil in a deep pan. Place stuffed peppers in face-down; cover
and cook for about 10 minutes until meat is browned slightly.
Add potatoes, celery and onion to pan; cover and cook another
15 minutes. Then flip the peppers right-side up. Add bouillon
and tomatoes to pot and stir to combine. Cover and let cook
over low heat about 30–45 minutes, or until potatoes are cooked
through.

Sprinkle peppers with parmesan cheese when ready to serve.

KRAUTWICKEL– stuffed cabbage

2 head green cabbage
2 ½ lb. ground pork
½ lb. short grained rice
Salt & pepper to taste
½ teaspoon sweet paprika
4 Yukon gold potatoes
3 to 4 strips bacon, chopped
1 medium yellow onion, chopped
2 chicken bouillon cubes

SERVES 8

Cut off one inch from the core side of one cabbage and rinse
remaining head under cold water. Pour two cups of water into a
two-quart pot. Place cabbage head core side on the bottom and
cook over medium heat with a lid on for about 20–30 minutes
until all the leaves easily peel off. Repeat with second cabbage.
Make certain not to overcook the leaves or they will tear when
filling them.

While cabbage is cooking, mix together the ground pork, rice,
salt & pepper, and paprika with your hand. Peel your potatoes
and set both components aside.

When cabbage is finished cooking, remove and begin peeling off
leaves. Lay leaves flat on working surface. Put a serving spoonful of pork mixture in the middle of each and envelope the meat
with the cabbage using the firmest part of the cabbage at the
base. Tuck in the sides.

In a Dutch oven, sauté the bacon and onion. Place the cabbage rolls in rows into the Dutch oven. Cut the peeled potatoes in quarters and lay on top of the rolls. Sprinkle the top with the crushed chicken bouillon cubes. Shred the second cabbage and spread over the potatoes. Season with salt & pepper to taste. Preheat oven to 350° F and place lidded Dutch oven in the oven for about an hour. Take the lid off and bake uncovered for another 15–20 minutes, until potatoes are soft and rice is tender.

GYULAI WURST MIT KRAUT – sausage & kraut

1 ½ lb. Hungarian sausages (2 pairs of Guylai sausages – spicy
or mild is up to you!)
2 lbs. sauerkraut (1 large jar)
1 cube chicken bouillon
1 tablespoon caraway seeds

SERVES 6

In a shallow pan place the sausages, and fill with water so that
the sausages are half covered. Cook on medium heat. Bring
to a boil and let simmer for 30 minutes. Pour off the liquid.
Pour the sauerkraut into a bowl and submerge in cold water.
Rinse completely squeezing out all the excess moisture. Repeat
once more. Add the sauerkraut to the sausage. Crumble a cube
chicken bouillon and add 1½ cups water. Sprinkle the caraway
seeds on top. Let this cook for another 30 minutes on medium
heat.

Take the sausage out and cut in one-inch pieces. Put back into
the bed of kraut and let simmer for another 30 minutes. This
allows the juices from the sausage to seep into the kraut. Serve
with either mashed or boiled potatoes.

KÖNIGSBERGER KLOPS – meatballs bohemian style

1 ½ lbs. ground beef
1 ½ lbs. ground pork
1 slice of day-old bread
Salt & pepper
2 medium yellow onions
4 anchovy fillets – chopped
1 egg
2 tablespoons canola oil
1 beef bouillon cube
2 tablespoons flour
½ cup crème fraiche
½-ish cup of dry, white wine – a *Schuck*

SERVES 6

Combine beef and pork in large mixing bowl. Season with salt
& pepper. Soak bread in water or milk, squeeze out excess
liquid and crumble into meat mixture. Dice 1 onion and add to
mixture. Add anchovies and egg, and mix by hand to incorporate. If mixture feels a little dry to the touch, add a small amount
of water or milk until mixture is the consistency of hamburger
meat. Don't over-mix or *Klops* will get tough.

Heat oil in large, heavy skillet. Form meatball-sized balls by
hand and place into pan. Brown on all sides (about 6–8 minutes
per side).

Add remaining onion, chopped, and sauté with meat until
browned. Sprinkle bouillon cube into pan, mix flour and crème
fraiche together and then add small amount of warm water and

stir to incorporate in the pan. Slowly add 1 cup of warm water. Cover pan and simmer for 20–30 minutes. Finish sauce with a *Schuck* of dry, white wine.

Serve with mashed potatoes, *Spätzle* or egg noodles.

ROULADEN – steak rolls

1 ½ lbs. sandwich steak – sliced thinly
Salt & pepper
Garlic salt
6 slices uncooked bacon – chopped
1 large onion – sliced thinly
3 carrots – julienned
3 stalks celery – julienned
2 tablespoon fresh parsley – chopped
1 cube beef bouillon
1 cup dry red wine – divided

SERVES 6

Cut steak slices into portion-sized pieces (about the size of your hand). Sprinkle with salt, pepper and garlic salt. Add about 4 slices chopped bacon, dividing evenly among steak portions (reserving remaining bacon for later). Place 3–4 slices each of onion, carrot and celery onto each steak (reserve some of each for the sauce). Roll steaks up and secure with a toothpick to close.

In a Dutch oven or large, deep pan, brown remaining bacon; then add rolled steaks to pan, browning on all sides. Cover pan between turns of the meat so that steaks don't stick to the bottom of the pan. Once steaks are browned, add remaining onion, carrot, celery and parsley and sprinkle one cube of beef bouillon cube. Cover pan and cook over medium-high heat until vegetables are tender (about 30 minutes).

Add ½ cup warm water mixed with ½ cup dry, red wine to pan

and stir to incorporate pan juices. Cover and cook a further 30 minutes; then add another ½ cup of warm water mixed with ½ cup of red wine. (If you like your sauce thicker, sprinkle 1 table-spoon flour over the veggies before you add the last water and wine). Cover and simmer for another 30 minutes. Meat should be nice and tender.

VEGETABLES, SOUPS & SALADS

RÖSTI KARTOFFELN – roasted cheesy potatoes

6 medium potatoes
6 bacon strips (lean)
1 tablespoon canola oil
1 cup gruyere cheese grated (buy it whole and grate it
yourself – much better flavor)

SERVES 6

Boil the potatoes with the skin on until fully cooked. Pour off
the water and let them cool slightly. Peel the potatoes and press
them through a ricer into a bowl and let them sit for a moment
covered. In the meantime, dice your bacon strips and then fry
in a large skillet, preferably a cast iron skillet (it makes a nicer
crust). Take the bacon pieces out and leave the bacon fat in the
pan.

In that same skillet, add the tablespoon oil and press the potatoes into the pan. On medium heat, press the potatoes down and
allow the potatoes to brown lightly on the bottom. Should be
about 10 minutes. Lift up a side with your spatula – you want a
nice golden brown color.

Spread the bacon bits on one half of the potatoes. Add the grated
gruyere on the half with the bacon. Using two spatulas, gently
flip the other side of the potatoes over to cover the bacon and
gruyere, similar to an omelet. Let cook until the cheese has
melted – another 8 minutes or so. Slide the potato *"Rösti"* onto a
warm platter. Makes a great breakfast/brunch dish with eggs or a
light salad.

KARTOFFELPFANNKUCHEN – potato pancakes, sweet or savory

4 lbs. Idaho baking potatoes
1 lemon
3 eggs
1 ¼ cup breadcrumbs
½ cup vegetable oil or Crisco

SERVES 8

Peel potatoes and rinse quickly with cold water. Towel dry.
Sprinkle potatoes with lemon juice. In large bowl grate the potatoes using the largest grate setting. Add lemon juice occasionally
to keep potatoes from turning brown. If mixture is too liquidy,
line a colander with cheesecloth and set mixture inside, draining
the excess liquid. When all potatoes are grated and dried, add
eggs and breadcrumbs and mix by hand.

Drizzle some oil (or Crisco – maybe 2 tablespoons) in a large
hot skillet. When the oil is hot, drop about a serving spoonful
of batter into pan and flatten with a spoon. They should have an
oval shape about the size of your hand. You should be able to
fit 3 such pancakes in a skillet. Flip them over when browned
on bottom. Remove when other side is browned. Add oil to pan
as needed when making pancakes. Serve warm with any or all:
melted cheese, applesauce, sour cream or maple syrup.

WEISER SPARGEL MIT KREME SOSSE –
white asparagus with cream sauce

1 tablespoon butter or margarine
1 tablespoon flour
1 cup milk (cream is better, but also richer)
½ chicken bouillon
Salt & pepper to taste
½ teaspoon nutmeg (ground)(grate it yourself from a whole
nutmeg –much richer flavor)
2 cans or jars of white asparagus

SERVES 4–6

In a saucepan, melt the butter over medium heat. Add the
flour and stir creating a roux – don't let this mixture get dark.
Crumble the bouillon into the roux. Gradually, add milk and let
this mixture come to a boil. You need to constantly stir with a
wooden spoon or it will clump up on you. Add salt & pepper and
the nutmeg, stirring constantly. Take the asparagus and pour off
all the excess liquid. Add the asparagus stalks to this mixture.
Take it off medium heat and let it heat through on low heat.
When ready to serve, grate an extra bit of nutmeg over the top.
This dish goes wonderfully with pork or poultry.

BLUMENKOHLSALAT – cauliflower salad

1 head cauliflower, trimmed & cut into bite-sized pieces
1 cup water
1 small onion
¼ cup "Salada" or other salad vinegar
Salt
Pepper
¼ cup vegetable or canola oil
1 tablespoon mayonnaise

SERVES 4–6

Place cauliflower and water into medium saucepan and bring
water to boil. Then reduce heat and steam until cauliflower is
soft, but still crunchy. When you poke it with a fork it should
resist a bit. It should easily break into florets. Drain liquid from
pan. Place cauliflower in bowl and add the onion, sliced thinly.
Mix vinegar, salt, pepper, oil and mayo to form a dressing and
pour over cauliflower. Let rest at room temperature, stirring
occasionally. If desired, warm in oven before serving.

ROSENKOHLSALAT – Brussels sprout salad

1 ½ lbs. fresh Brussels sprouts
2 tablespoon canola oil
1 small onion, chopped
1 chicken bouillon cube
¼ cup "Salata" or other salad vinegar
Salt & pepper

SERVES 4–6

Rinse sprouts and dry on paper towel. Remove stem and slice in half length-wise. In a medium skillet, heat the oil, add sprouts and sauté gently until lightly browned and tender. Add onion and incorporate. Continue cooking until onions are slightly translucent. Sprinkle chicken bouillon into pan and add ¼ cup warm water, along with the vinegar. Stir and add salt & pepper to taste. Simmer over low heat until al dente (about 10–15 minutes longer).

ROTE BEETE SALAT – red beet salad

4 fresh red beets – approximately the same sized (buy it with the green stalk still attached – keeps the flavor longer)
1 white onion
1 clove garlic – minced or diced finely
Salt & pepper to taste
2 tablespoons vinegar
2 tablespoons olive oil
1 teaspoon horseradish

SERVES 4–6

Boil the beets in water until fully cooked. With a fork they should pierce easily. Pour off the water and let the beets rest for two minutes on a paper towel. Take two pieces of aluminum foil in your hands almost like catcher's mitts. Take each beet and with one hand moving clockwise and the other moving counter-clockwise, gently scrape off the skin of each beet – (this will peel off really smoothly and also avoid getting red stains on everything).

Place the beets on a cutting board. (Prep the board first by putting on a thin coating of olive oil). Cut each beet in half and then slice into bite size pieces. Put in a bowl. Slice your onion thin and add to beets. Dice/mince your garlic and add to beets. Add salt, pepper, vinegar, olive oil and horseradish. Mix together so that all your beets are fully coated. Can be served either warm or cold the next day!

MÖRENSALAT – carrot and celery root salad

1 large celery root
6 carrots
1 yellow onion
Salt & pepper to taste
1 tablespoon fresh parsley
2 tablespoons vinegar
2 tablespoons olive oil

SERVES 4–6

Boil unpeeled celery root in a medium saucepan. In a separate pot, boil the unpeeled carrots. When the vegetables are easily pierced with a fork, drain out the water. Let the vegetables cool and then peel. Slice the carrots diagonally into a bowl. Cut the celery root into quarters and then into bite sized pieces. Add salt & pepper. Mix the vinegar and oil with the parsley and then pour over the carrots and celery root. Toss lightly. May be served warm or cold.

GURKENSALAT – cucumber salad

2 seedless cucumbers
4 slices Canadian bacon
2 tablespoon vegetable oil – divided
1 medium yellow onion
1 teaspoon fresh dill, chopped
½ teaspoon sugar
Salt & freshly ground white pepper
3 tablespoon "Salata" or other salad vinegar

SERVES 4–6

Peel cucumbers and slice thinly using grater on mandolin setting.
Place sliced cucumbers into bowl and salt lightly – set aside.
Before adding other ingredients, drain excess water. Meanwhile,
in a medium pan, sauté Canadian bacon in 1 teaspoon oil until
browned. Chop onion finely and pour over cucumber slices.
Then add browned bacon. Top salad with dill. Finish with
vinegar, remaining vegetable oil; and season with salt & white
pepper to taste. Serve immediately.

KARTOFFELSALAT – potato salad

6 medium Yukon gold potatoes
Salt & pepper to taste
3 strips lean bacon, cut in julienne slices
¼ cup salad oil (canola will also work)
1 yellow onion – diced
1 cube chicken bullion
1 tablespoon flour
½ teaspoon sugar
¼ cup vinegar

SERVES 6

Boil potatoes until fully cooked. Drain the water and peel. Cut in half lengthwise and then cut them thinly across into bite size pieces. Sprinkle with salt & pepper. Set aside. In sauté pan, crisp the bacon and when nice and crunchy, pour the contents of pan over the potatoes including the bacon fat. Add oil to the pan, melt the two and add the diced onions. Sauté the onions, when translucent, crumble the bouillon and flour onto the onions and stir with a wooden spoon. Slowly drizzle about a cup of water into the onion mixture to make a roux. Add the sugar. Slowly add the vinegar and let the entire mixture SLIGHTLY bubble. Turn off the heat and pour over the potatoes. Let it sit for about 5 minutes and then toss gently with two wooden spoons. Best when served warm! Can be reheated the next day, if needed.

LINSEN SUPPE –lentil soup

1 lb dried lentils (brown or red)
2 bay leaves
6 new potatoes
2 small yellow onions
2 carrots
2 stalks celery
1 tablespoon butter
2 bouillon cube (chicken or vegetable)
Salt & pepper
2 tablespoon vinegar
Dollop sour cream (if desired)
Chopped green onions (also, if desired – or add them both!)

SERVES 6–8

Pour lentils into medium/large saucepan and cover with twice
as much water as lentils. Add bay leaves. Bring to boil over
medium-high heat, then remove from heat and let rest for 2 hours.

Meanwhile, chop potatoes, onions, carrots and celery into bite-
size pieces. Add all except the onions to the lentils and resume
cooking over medium heat, stirring occasionally. Soup is nearly
done when potatoes and vegetables are cooked through (about
45 minutes to an hour).

In a separate skillet, sauté onions in butter. Once onions are
translucent, add the crumbled chicken or vegetable bouillon
cubes to center of skillet and sauté with onions. Slowly pour in
a ladle full of the cooking lentil soup and cook briefly. Then add
onion mixture to soup.

Salt & pepper soup to taste and add 2 tablespoon vinegar before serving, if desired. You can add a dollop of sour cream on the top with chopped green onions!

DESSERTS

LENI'S APFELSCHNITTEN – apple slices

2 ½ sticks butter
3 cups flour
3 eggs (separated)
2/3 cup sugar
3 tablespoon sour cream
1 tablespoon vinegar
1 tablespoon vanilla extract
Bread crumbs as needed to soak up excess liquid from apples
10 apples (preferably Granny Smith or McIntosh)
¼ cup course ground sugar

Dice butter into flour and mix gently by hand into crumbs.
In another bowl, mix together egg yolks, sugar, sour cream,
vinegar and vanilla with hand mixer on low setting. Reserve egg
whites and set aside. Add egg yolk mixture slowly to the flour/
butter mixture and knead by hand until dough comes easily off
hands and side of bowl. Form dough into a ball, place in a deep
bowl. Cover with plastic wrap and refrigerate for 1 hour.
(This step may be done up to a day ahead).

Remove refrigerated dough. Sprinkle a large cutting board with
flour. Take half the dough mixture and roll out on board to size
of a cookie sheet (about 11x16"). Grease cookie sheet with
butter. Keep rolling pin and board well-floured to prevent
sticking. When dough is rolled to correct size, roll onto rolling
pin and then roll out onto greased cookie sheet. Press dough
as needed into sides and edges of pan. Sprinkle with a little
bread crumbs.

Peel and slice apples thinly; then layer these onto the prepared dough. Sprinkle a little sugar and/or raisins if you like. Take out remaining dough and roll-out as above, but to a slightly larger size. Roll second half of dough on top of apples so entire pan is covered. Seal at edges, then pierce dough with fork to allow air flow.

In a small bowl, beat the egg whites until fluffy, with a pinch of salt. Brush over top layer of dough; then sprinkle with course-ground sugar. Bake at 350° F for 1 hour. Remove from oven and allow to cool slightly before serving.

OMA'S PFLAUMENKUCHEN – plum cake

3 ½ cups flour
½ cup sugar – divided
1 packet yeast
3 egg yolks
A pinch of salt
1 ¼ cups milk – warmed to 110° F
1 tablespoon butter or margarine – to butter the pan
30 Italian plums (sometimes called prune plums – the other varieties are too watery for this dish – NOTE these are usually only available in late summer)
½ cup sugar

About an hour before preparing dough, take out the eggs, milk and butter so that all ingredients are at room temperature. Put 3 cups flour into bowl and scoop out a well in the middle of the flour. Sprinkle 1 tablespoon sugar into well. Empty contents of yeast packet into same well. In a separate bowl take 3 egg yolks and add the salt and the remaining sugar and mix well so that sugar, salt and eggs are fully incorporated. Warm the milk on the stove to about 110° F or slightly warm when you sprinkle a bit on your wrist.

When milk is warmed pour about ¼ cup into the well and begin stirring slowly with your finger keeping the walls of the well intact. You want to fully incorporate the yeast, sugar, milk and a bit of the flour so that you have a lump-free slurry. DO NOT incorporate all the flour! Just the bit that's in the well. Once you have the slurry lump-free, toss a little of the flour over it and let sit until you see cracks forming in the well. (About 5–7 minutes).

Add the egg yolk mixture to the flour by pouring it along the outside rim of the flour mixture and slowly add a little of the milk. Begin to work the dough with your hands. (You can do this with a wooden spoon – however, you really get better results in terms of airiness and a great "feel" for the dough if this is done by hand). The dough will be wet – as you are incorporating more and more of the flour also drizzle in the milk. Keep kneading the dough, scooping it from the bottom and folding over the top. This is where you may need to sprinkle a bit more flour into your dough, no more that ½ cup.

Once the dough has a nice smooth surface, and the dough comes off cleanly from your fingers, the dough is ready to "rest." Place the dough in the middle of your bowl and then slightly oil the inside walls of the bowl so that when the dough rises it won't stick to the sides. Cover the bowl with a lint-free towel and then on top of that put a heavier bath towel to keep the dough warm. Keep the dough in a warm draft-free place (I usually pre-set the oven to 350° F and then turn it off – once the oven is beginning to cool, I place the bowl with dough and towels inside to rise) MAKE SURE OVEN IS OFF WHEN YOU DO THIS!!!

Let the dough rise for about an hour and 15 minutes. Flour a large wooden baking board. Put the dough into the middle and then roll it out to about a ½-inch thickness. Roll out the dough onto a rimmed baking sheet. With a fork, pierce the dough throughout.

While the dough is rising, rinse your plums and prepare the plums. Cut each plum along its seam. Do not cut the plum all the way through. Remove the stone. Layer the plums onto the dough overlapping the plums to fully cover. Bake at 350° F in pre-heated oven for 30–40 minutes. Once the rim is golden brown, the cake is ready. When cake has cooled – the plums are cool to your touch, sprinkle the sugar over the top.

OMA'S STREUSELKUCHEN – Streusel coffee cake

3 ½ cups flour
½ cup sugar – divided
1 packet yeast
3 egg yolks
A pinch of salt
1 ¼ cups milk – warmed to 110° F
1 tablespoon butter or margarine to butter the pan

For Streusel topping:
1 cup sugar
1 cup flour
1 stick butter or margarine

For Custard:
2 eggs
2 cups sour cream
2 tablespoons sugar
1 teaspoon flour

About an hour before preparing dough, take out the eggs, milk and butter so that all ingredients are at room temperature. Put 3 cups flour into bowl and scoop out a well in the middle of the flour. Sprinkle one tablespoon sugar and yeast packet into well. In a separate bowl take 3 egg yolks and add the salt and the remaining sugar and mix well so that sugar, salt and eggs are fully incorporated. Warm the milk on the stove to about 110° F or slightly warm when you sprinkle a bit on your wrist.

When milk is warmed pour about ¼ cup into the well and begin stirring slowly with your finger keeping the walls of the well intact. You want to fully incorporate the yeast, sugar, milk and a bit of the flour so that you have a lump-free slurry. DO NOT incorporate all the flour! Just the bit that's in the well. Once you have the slurry lump-free, toss a little of the flour over it and let sit until you see cracks forming in the well. (About 5–7 minutes).

Add the egg yolk mixture by pouring it along the outside rim of the flour mixture and slowly add a little of the milk. Begin to work the dough with your hands. (You can do this with a wooden spoon – however, you really get better results in terms of airiness and a great "feel" for the dough if this is done by hand). The dough will be wet – as you are incorporating more and more of the flour also drizzle in the milk. Keep kneading the dough, scooping it from the bottom and folding over the top. This is where you may need to sprinkle a bit more flour into your dough, no more that ½ cup.

Once the dough has a nice smooth surface, and the dough comes off cleanly from your fingers, the dough is ready to "rest." Place the dough in the middle of your bowl and then slightly oil the inside walls of the bowl so that when the dough rises it won't stick to the sides. Cover the bowl with a lint-free towel and then on top of that put a heavier bath towel to keep the dough warm. Keep the dough in a warm place (I usually pre-set an oven to 350° F and then turn it off – once the oven is beginning to cool, I place the bowl with dough and towels inside to rise) MAKE SURE OVEN IS OFF WHEN YOU DO THIS!!!

Let the dough rise for about an hour and 15 minutes. Flour a large wooden baking board. Put the dough into the middle and then roll it out to about a ½-inch thickness. Roll out the dough onto a rimmed baking sheet. With a fork, pierce the dough throughout.

While dough is rising prepare the *Streusel* by taking the 1 cup sugar, flour and cooled stick of butter and combine with hand until it forms a nice crumble. Refrigerate. For custard, combine 2 eggs, 2 cup sour cream, 2 tablespoons sugar and 1 teaspoon flour. Pour this mixture over the top of the dough. Take out the *Streusel* and crumble it over the egg/sour cream mixture. Evenly distribute the *Streusel* avoiding the rims. Bake at 350° F for 30–40 minutes, until the rim is golden brown. Ready to serve warm or cold.

TANTE MARGRET'S APFELMUSSKUCHEN – applesauce cake

½ cup shortening

2 cups sugar

1 egg

2 ½ cups flour

1 ½ teaspoon baking soda

1 ½ teaspoon salt

¾ teaspoon cinnamon

½ teaspoon allspice

½ teaspoon ground cloves

½ cup water

1 ½ cups applesauce

½ cup chopped walnuts

½ cup golden raisins

Melt shortening over low heat. Mix all other ingredients together in mixing bowl and add shortening; mix to incorporate. Pour into greased and floured bundt cake pan or bread loaf pan (or 13x9x2 rectangle). Bake at 350° F for 35–40 minutes. Serve alone or with a scoop of ice cream or dollop of whipped cream.

OBST KOMPOTT – fruit compote

5–6 medium apples, peeled, cored & cut into chunks (or whatever seasonal fruit is available – you can do a combination as
well with berries, plums, and apples)
½ cup cold water
2 tablespoon sugar
½ cup raisins
2 tablespoon light rum

Place chunked apples (fruit) into medium saucepan, add
water and cook over medium heat. After 30 minutes, add 2
tablespoons sugar and simmer over low heat. Add raisins and
rum and simmer until raisins plump. Remove from heat and
allow to cool to room temperature. Serve with vanilla ice
cream – yogurt – cottage cheese – *Schmarren* – crepes – or just
plain out of the bowl!

FRAU SCHOEPKO'S RICE PUDDING WITH APRICOTS

2 eggs
3 cups milk
1 ½ cup short grained rice
½ cup sugar
3 teaspoon corn starch
Pinch of salt
¼ cup chopped, dried apricots
1 teaspoon vanilla
1 pint whipped cream
½ cups sugar

Lightly beat eggs and set aside. In a large saucepan, bring milk to a boil then add rice and cook, stirring over medium heat until mixture thickens. Blend eggs, sugar, corn starch, salt, apricots and vanilla together adding a ladle of milk from the rice to make a nice creamy mixture. Gradually add this slowly to the rice and stir so that nothing sticks to the bottom. Let this simmer on low heat for about 10 minutes. Rice should be nice and soft. Let the rice cool. In a separate bowl whip together the whipped cream and sugar and then fold into the cold rice mixture. Top with sprinkled cinnamon, if desired.

LIZ'S TAFFY APPLE SALAD

2 cups mini-marshmallows
1 large can of chunk pineapples (drain and reserve the juice)
1 tablespoon flour
½ cup sugar
1 ½ tablespoon white vinegar
1 egg, lightly beaten
1 8 oz Cool Whip (or you can combine ½ cup Cool Whip &
½ cup sour cream)
2 cups unpeeled apples, chopped (your choice – Granny Smith
will give you a more tart contrast)
1 ½ cup cocktail peanuts or almonds

Mix marshmallows and pineapples. Refrigerate overnight. In a
medium saucepan combine pineapple juice, flour, sugar, vinegar
and egg and cook until you have a nice thick sauce. Refrigerate
overnight. Next day combine Cool Whip with pineapple/marsh-
mallow mixture and sauce mixture, then fold in apples and nuts.
Ready to serve! The kids will love this and they can help put this
one together!

OBST TORTE – seasonal fruit torte

1 stick butter
1 ½ cups flour
1 whole egg and 1 yolk
1/3 cup sugar
1 tablespoon sour cream
1 teaspoon brandy
1 teaspoon vanilla extract
1/2 pint blueberries
1/2 pint strawberries
1/2 pint raspberries
1/2 pint blackberries
1 tablespoon either apple or currant jelly
Glaze: 1 package Dr. Oetker's clear glaze (best results)

Dice butter into flour and mix gently by hand into crumbs. In another bowl, mix together egg yolks, sugar, sour cream, brandy and vanilla with hand mixer on low setting. Reserve egg white and set aside. Add egg yolk mixture slowly to the flour/butter mixture and knead by hand until dough comes easily off hands and side of bowl. Form dough into a ball, place in a deep bowl, cover with plastic wrap and refrigerate for 1 hour. (This step may be done up to a day ahead).

Remove refrigerated dough. Sprinkle a large cutting board with flour. Roll out on board to fit either a pie tin or spring-form pan. (I opt for the spring pan – comes out nicer) Grease pan with butter. Press dough with two fingers to the side to make a nice lip to hold the fruit. Prick the bottom of the dough with a fork. Place in oven at 350° F for 20–30 minutes until the dough is golden brown.

In the meantime, rinse and paper towel dry your fruit. De-stem the strawberries and slice them in half. When your dough is golden brown allow it to cool for about 10 minutes. Spread the jelly onto the bottom of the cake. Starting with the outside circle, place the blackberries one row deep. The next circle should be blueberries (1 or 2 rows, depending on your liking) then one row of raspberries and then fill the middle with the strawberries. You can get fancy by creating a nice flower form with the halved strawberries. Prepare the glaze according to the directions and then spoon evenly over the fruit. Allow to set for 20–30 minutes – ready to serve. We serve this torte with either whipped cream or Cool Whip.

MR. McKAY'S (from St. Lambert's) CHEESECAKE

For crust:
2 cups graham cracker crumbs
½ cup sugar
1 ½ teaspoon cinnamon
¼ cup melted, unsalted butter

For filling:
6 eggs, separated
1 cup sugar
2 12 oz. cream cheeses
3 tablespoon tapioca pudding mix (regular)
1 16-oz sour cream
1 teaspoon vanilla
1 teaspoon lemon juice

Combine crust ingredients by hand. Grease a spring-form pan with butter; then press ¾ of crumb mixture onto bottom and sides of pan. Set aside.

Separate eggs and set egg whites aside. In a large mixing bowl, combine egg yolks with sugar, cream cheese, tapioca, sour cream, vanilla and lemon juice with hand mixer on medium until smooth. In a separate bowl, whip egg whites until peaks form. Then fold egg whites into filling mixture gently with a spatula. Pour filling mixture into prepared pan and crumble remaining crust/topping over the top.

Bake in a pre-heated 300° F oven for 1 ½ hours. Then turn oven off and leave cake inside for another hour. Remove and let cool; then refrigerate overnight before serving.

OPA SUDENDORF'S CREAM PUFFS

For puffs:
1 cup cold water
1 stick butter
½ teaspoon salt
1 cup flour
4 eggs

For filling
1 ½ cup sour cherries (or any desired fruit filling)
1 pint cream for whipping
½ cup sugar

Confectioner's sugar to sprinkle

In a medium saucepan heat water, butter and salt over medium-low heat, until butter melts. Add flour stirring constantly with a wooden spoon until dough forms a ball. Remove from heat. Add eggs, one at a time combining with wooden spoon, mixing thoroughly until dough is shiny.

Drop rounded tablespoons of dough onto ungreased cookie sheet. You can also use a pastry bag with a round setting. Bake at 350° F for approximately 10–15 minutes, or until dough is golden brown. When cooled, slice neatly in half but not all the way through. Fill with sour cherries. Whip sugar and 1 pint whipped cream together. Add a dollop of whipped cream over the sour cherries. Sprinkle lightly with powdered sugar.

Felizitas Sudendorf

SEASONAL DISHES

BETTY BACHMEIER'S CHRIST STOLLEN

Dough mixture:
9 cups flour
4 packages dry yeast
2 ¼ cup milk – divided
5 eggs (2 whole and 3 yolks)
2 sticks butter (set aside at room temperature)
1 tablespoon oil or Crisco
1 cup sugar
pinch of salt

Topping:
½ cup dried cherries
½ cup light raisins
¼ cup candied orange
¼ cup candied lemon
½ cup chopped pecans
½ cup chopped almonds
1 package vanilla sugar
1 lemon (juice and zest)
1 orange (juice and zest)
1 tablespoon almond extract
1 tablespoon Stroh Rum

---

1 stick butter
1 cup powdered sugar

Put flour in a big bowl. In the middle make a dent and sprinkle in the yeast. Heat milk to 110° F. Don't let milk get too hot. Add a spoonful of sugar onto the yeast then add ½ cup of warm milk into the dent stirring to make a small paste. Sprinkle a little flour over the top then set aside.

In another bowl mix all the remaining ingredients (except for the stick of butter and 1 cup confectioner's sugar) raisin/nut/fruit ingredients with the liquids, allowing this mixture to soak. Cover and set aside.

When the dough begins to crack from the yeast add the eggs, butter dropped in small pieces, oil/Crisco, sugar and pinch of salt and knead the dough until it comes off easily from your hands. Place in a bowl in a warm place covered with plastic wrap and a warm towel for about an hour. Prepare cutting board (I usually use two placed side by side) by sprinkling with flour.

Place the risen dough on the board and flatten with your hands. Coat the soaked raisin nut mixture drained of the liquid with a little flour so they don't stick to each other then pour on top of the dough and knead it all together. Divide into four pieces and form into balls. Flatten each with your hand. They should each be the size of a 2 inch thick dinner plate. Flip one side over like an omelet, but let the bottom lip protrude more than the flipped over side. Place each loaf on a parchment lined cookie sheet for one hour to rise to double its size. Place in 350° F oven on middle rack for one hour. When golden brown remove from oven and immediately brush with melted butter. Sprinkle liberally with powdered sugar.

Frohe Weihnachten!

MARGRET TRAUB'S JULIANA SCHNITTEN – nut bars

For crust:
1 ¾ cups flour
1 ½ stick butter – softened at room temperature
½ cup sugar
1 lemon peel
2 egg yolks
2 tablespoon sour cream
¼ teaspoon baking powder
Apricot marmalade

For filling:
4 cups freshly ground nuts (walnuts or pecans are best – if you can't find them freshly ground buy them whole and grind them in your coffee grinder)
1 ½ cups sugar
¾ cups breadcrumbs
1 packet vanilla sugar
8 egg whites – beaten
1 teaspoon baking powder
½ cup cold milk

For glaze:
¾ cup powder sugar
Juice of one lemon

Mix together flour, butter and sugar until fully incorporated. Next add lemon peel, egg yolks, sour cream and baking powder until all the components are also well incorporated. Form the dough into a smooth ball. Press the ball into a buttered baking sheet with a high rim. Spread a thin layer of apricot marmalade over the top and set aside.

In a separate bowl mix together the nuts, sugar, breadcrumbs, vanilla sugar, and beaten egg whites with mixer. Add the baking powder. When everything is well incorporated, add the cold milk. Spread this mixture over the top of your dough. Bake in 350° F oven for 45 – to 50 minutes.

To make the glaze, mix the powder sugar with the lemon and brush onto the top of the warm *Schnitten*. When cooled, cut into bars, squares, whatever shape you prefer! We have these at Christmas – but any special occasion will do!

SPRITZGEBÄCK – pressed butter cookies

2 ½ sticks butter
3 cups flour
3 eggs (yolks only)
1 cup sugar
1 tablespoon sour cream
1 tablespoon vinegar
1 tablespoon vanilla extract

Dice butter into flour and mix gently by hand into crumbs. In another bowl, mix together egg yolks, sugar, sour cream, vinegar and vanilla with hand mixer on low setting.

Add egg yolk mixture slowly to the flour/butter mixture and knead by hand until dough comes easily off hands and the side of bowl.* Form dough into a ball, place in a deep bowl, cover with plastic wrap and refrigerate for 1 hour. (This step may be done up to a day ahead).

Remove refrigerated dough. Sprinkle a large cutting board with flour. Take the dough mixture and form into a long roll about the size of a French baguette. Cut the roll into 2–3 inch pieces. Attach the meat grinder to your table with the star cookie attachment. (If you don't have a meat grinder, roll out the dough very thinly and cut out with cookie cutters). Feed the dough into the grinder and make 3-inch pieces. Take each piece and form into a circle. You can also form them into candy canes for a change, or just keep them as straight logs. Place the formed cookies on an ungreased cookie sheet. You can also place them on parchment paper if that is your preferred way of baking.

Place 350° F oven for 5–10 minutes until bottoms are lightly golden. The top should still be light. When you take them out of the oven roll them into either granulated sugar or dip half the cookie into chocolate (Take your favorite chocolate bar and melt) or a vanilla and lemon glaze – you can dress these as you would a sugar cookie. Let cool.

* For a variation; add one tablespoon of cocoa powder to the dough as you are kneading it for a nice light chocolate flavor.

PATTI'S CARMELITAS

For crust:
1 ½ cup flour
1 ½ cup oatmeal
¾ cup brown sugar
½ teaspoon baking soda
Pinch salt
2 sticks butter

For filling:
3 tablespoon flour
12 oz. caramel topping
1 bag semi-sweet chocolate chips
1 cup chopped nuts – whatever you like best – I like pecans!

Preheat oven to 375° F

Mix together flour, oatmeal, brown sugar, baking soda and salt. Melt butter and pour into dry mixture. Mix flour together until nice crumbly consistency. Take ¾ crust mixture and press into bottom of Pyrex dish making certain it's evenly distributed. Place in oven for about 12–15 minutes, until lightly brown. Remove from oven and let cool.

In the meantime, add 3 tablespoons flour to caramel topping mix and set aside. After you've removed the crust pour chocolate chips and nuts onto crust distributing evenly. Drizzle caramel mixture over the crust and then finally sprinkle the remaining crust dough over the top. Return to oven and bake for additional 20 minutes until top is golden brown. Let cool, scraping sides of pan so caramel and chocolate doesn't stick.

When cooled, cut into bars. You can save these for about a month.

FASCHING'S KRAPFEN – (Paczki's) Lenten Bismarcks

6 cups flour (with possibly ½ cup more as "kneaded")
3 tablespoons sugar – divided
1 packet yeast
5 egg yolks
½ teaspoon salt
2 ½ cups milk – warmed to 110° F
1 tablespoon butter or margarine
2–3 cups vegetable oil for frying – enough for the *Krapfen* to "swim" no touching the bottom!
1 cup powdered sugar
Fruit marmalade – orange, mixed fruit, pick your favorite!

About an hour before preparing dough, take out the eggs, milk and butter so that all ingredients are at room temperature. Put 6 cups flour into bowl and scoop out a well in the middle of the flour. Sprinkle 1 tablespoon sugar into well. Empty contents of yeast packet into same well. In a separate bowl take 5 egg yolks and add the ½ teaspoon salt and 2 tablespoons sugar and butter/margarine at room temperature. Mix well so that sugar, salt and eggs are fully incorporated. Warm the milk on the stove to about 110° F or slightly warm when you sprinkle a bit on your wrist.

When milk is warmed pour about ¼ cup into the well and begin stirring slowly with your finger keeping the walls of the well intact. You want to fully incorporate the yeast, sugar, milk and a bit of the flour so that you have a lump-free slurry. DO NOT incorporate all the flour! Just the bit that's in the well you made. Once you have the slurry lump-free, toss a little of the flour over it and let sit until you see cracks forming in the well. (About 5–7 minutes).

Add the egg yolk mixture by pouring it along the outside rim
of the flour mixture and slowly add a little of the milk. Begin
to work the dough with your hands. (You can do this with a
wooden spoon – however, you really get better results in terms
of airiness and a great "feel" for the dough if this is done by
hand). The dough will be wet – as you are incorporating more
and more of the flour also drizzle in the milk. Keep kneading
the dough, scooping it from the bottom and folding over the top.
This is where you may need to sprinkle a bit more flour into your
dough, no more that ½ cup.

Once the dough has a nice smooth surface, and the dough comes
off cleanly from your fingers, the dough is ready to "rest." Place
the dough in the middle of your bowl and then slightly oil the
inside walls of the bowl so that when the dough rises it won't
stick to the sides. Cover the bowl with a lint-free towel and then
on top of that put a heavier bath towel to keep the dough warm.
Keep the dough in a warm place (I usually pre-set an oven to
350° F and then turn it off – once the oven is beginning to cool,
I place the bowl with dough and towels inside to rise) MAKE
SURE OVEN IS OFF WHEN YOU DO THIS!!!

After the dough has rested for about an hour and fifteen minutes,
take it out of the bowl and place on floured surface – preferably
a wooden board. Flour your hands and rolling pin and roll out
the dough to about ½ inch to 1 inch thickness. Cut out 2 inch
rounds and set aside on floured surface. Should yield about 40–44
Krapfen. Place a lint-free towel over the rounds and let rest for
another 15 minutes.

Heat oil in a large pot. When oil is hot (you'll know when

you sprinkle a little water into the oil and it sputters) gently drop in 5–6 rounds depending on the size of your pot and let lightly brown. Turn over and let the other side lightly brown. Remove from oil and place in dish. Repeat for each *Krapfen*. When slightly cooled, sprinkle powdered sugar over the top. You can also squirt in marmalade if you want something extra sweet – otherwise serve nice and warm. You can freeze these once they've cooled and re-warm in 350° F oven for 5–7 minutes.

FRAU MUELLER'S (Leni's mom's) HÖRNCHEN – crescent rolls

8–10 cups flour
3 packages of dry yeast
1 teaspoon sugar
4 cups milk – divided
5 eggs
5 egg yolks
3 sticks butter (room temperature)
Caraway seeds and/or coarse salt (optional)

About an hour before preparing dough, take out the eggs, milk and butter so that all ingredients are at room temperature. Heat the milk to about 110° F. Place 8 cups flour in a large bowl, put a dent in the middle of the flour with your fist. Pour in the yeast then add sugar. Add a cup of the milk then stir with a wooden spoon to create a nice slurry in the middle of the flour. When you have a nice paste in the middle sprinkle a little flour over the mixture and let sit.

In a separate bowl mix the five whole eggs with the five yolks together. When you start to see cracks forming in the yeast paste add the egg mixture along the sides of the flour, add in the soft butter in chunks with the remaining warm milk and start kneading the dough together. If the dough is too wet, add additional flour, up to 2 cups. Once the dough is fully kneaded, spread a little vegetable oil around the sides of the bowl and roll the dough once around so that it doesn't stick to the sides. Cover with plastic wrap and a warm towel and let sit for an hour in a warm location.

After an hour the dough should have doubled in size. Remove from bowl and set on a large floured cutting board. Roll it with your hands into a long Italian bread shape. Then cut the dough into 5 even portions. Take your first portion and roll it into a ball, then roll it out with a rolling pin into a round pizza-shape. With a knife or pizza cutter, cut it into 8 pizza slices (you should have 8 triangles). Then roll from the fattest part inward, pulling on the sides to form a croissant. Line them on a baking sheet so they don't touch. Repeat with each of the 5 portions.

Brush each *Hörnchen* with egg wash (egg and water mixed together). Sprinkle with either coarse salt and/or caraway seeds for a more savory roll, otherwise leave them plain. Bake in 350° F oven for 15 minutes. Serve with butter, jam or just plain. They're great for Sunday breakfast!

OSTER STRITZEL – Easter braided bread

8–10 cups flour
3 packages of dry yeast
1 cup sugar
4 cups milk
5 eggs
5 egg yolks
1 teaspoon vanilla extract
1 stick butter (room temperature)

About an hour before preparing dough, take out the eggs, milk and butter so that all ingredients are at room temperature. Heat the milk to about 110° F. Place 8 cups flour in a large bowl, put a dent in the middle of the flour with your fist. Pour in the yeast then add a teaspoon sugar. Add a cup of the milk then stir with a wooden spoon to create a nice slurry in the middle of the flour. When you have a nice paste in the middle sprinkle a little flour over the mixture and let sit.

In a separate bowl mix the five whole eggs with the five yolks together and the remaining sugar and the vanilla extract. When you start to see cracks forming in the yeast paste add the egg mixture along the sides of the flour, add in the soft butter in chunks with the remaining warm milk and start kneading the dough together. If the dough is too wet, add additional flour, up to 2 cups. Once the dough is fully kneaded, spread a little vegetable oil around the sides of the bowl and roll the dough once around so that it doesn't stick to the sides. Cover with plastic wrap and a warm towel and let sit for an hour in a warm location.

After an hour the dough should have doubled in size. Remove

from bowl and set on a large floured cutting board. Cut the dough into three evenly sized pieces. Roll each piece with your hand to form a long French bread shape. Do the same with the remaining two dough portions. Line up the three separate bread shapes and then begin braiding them pulling slightly as you go along. You should have equal thickness throughout the bread dough.

Line a large cookie sheet with parchment paper. Butter it slightly. Form a wreath with your braid. You should have a nice opening in the middle of the braid. Let the braid rise by placing a lint-free dish towel over it and put it in a warm place for 30 minutes. Brush the top with egg wash (egg and water mixture). Bake it at 350° F for about 45 minutes to an hour – but I keep checking. You want a nice golden brown all over. We use it as a nest at the Easter table by putting our colored Easter eggs in the middle – makes a beautiful, edible centerpiece!

GUTEN APPETIT!

Acknowledgements

I need to acknowledge my father's cousin, "Pater Hannes," or more formally, Dr. Johannes Florian Mueller, whose book, *Ostdeutsches Schicksal am Schwarzen Meer*, gave me details in providing the historical backdrop to this memoir.

I want to thank my children; Patti, Linda, Mia and Richard, my brothers, Adi and Al and my sister Perpetua for their constant support, for filling in the blanks and for giving this memoir more color. I also wish to acknowledge those friends, especially Margret Rivest, members of the St. Alphonsus Choir, especially Leni Unger, and Kathe Milliker for their enthusiasm and encouragement throughout this process. I most importantly want to thank all my relatives and friends old and new, who have helped me to overcome any doubts in finding my home at last.

In terms of the recipes, I must recognize Margret Rivest, Leni Unger, her mother Frau Mueller, Margret Traub, Betty Bachmeier, Liz Mueller, Frau Schoepko, Jim McKay, Eduard Sudendorf, Linda Ransford, Patti Sudendorf and most especially my mother Benigna Mueller for their delicious contributions.

Finally I would like to thank Rick and Bridget Kaempfer not only for their suggestions and review, but for showing us how to get this project completed! Thanks to all!